Chef on the Run
by
Diane Clement

Sunflower Publications Ltd., Vancouver, Canada

Sunflower Publications Ltd.,
1426 West 26th Avenue,
Vancouver, British Columbia

Canadian Cataloguing in Publication Data

Clement, Diane, 1936-
  Chef on the run

  Includes index.
  ISBN 0-88894-368-7

  1. Entertaining.   2. Menus.   3. Cookery.
I. Title.
TX731.C59   642'.4   C82-091281-6

Typeset by Domino-Link Graphic Communications Ltd.
Printed and bound in Canada by Mitchell Press Ltd.

Acknowledgements
Jack Bryan, for photographs.
Western Living Magazine for permission to reprint four menus and photographs.
Air Canada
Various suppliers, including The Flower Studio by Tracy MacIvor — a new direction in floral art; Marsha Madill of The Doll's House for drama dolls; Pam Williams of Au Chocolat for truffles.
Peter and Joan Cundill, Ross and Linda Davidson, Haik Gharibians, Maurice and Pat Clement and John and Sharon Woyat who allowed photography in their homes.
Liz Bryan, who edited copy and designed the book.
Doug and all our friends who ate it all.
David, Joel and Dad, for inspiration.
Published by Sunflower Publications Ltd., Vancouver.

To Jennifer and Rand

Chef on the Run

I love to entertain and giving elaborate dinner parties is one of my favourite ways. But my life is pretty hectic and, like most career women, I don't have unlimited time to spend in the kitchen. So over the years I've put together some elegant party menus with dishes that can be prepared days — or even weeks — ahead, but which don't skimp on quality of flavour or presentation. The recipes have been taste-tested time and time again, always with compliments, and have also been tried for ease of preparation by students at my cooking school. I can safely call them all infallible. With all the major dishes ready to pop into the oven or take from refrigerator or freezer, on the day of my party I can take off my apron and socialize with my guests, relaxed and confident that the dinner will be a success and the evening a memorable one.

The 16 menus presented in "Chef on the Run" include the most popular of the recipes I have served to family, friends and students over the past 20 years. They are versatile and can be streamlined to suit different occasions and different budgets. I'm super-conscious about health and keeping fit and trim so usually I watch calories pretty carefully. When I entertain, calories are not counted, so dieters, beware!

Successful dinner parties just don't happen. They take time, patience and careful planning. Here are some of the things I've learned over the years:

Dinner Party Planning

Invite your guests at least three weeks ahead to avoid conflicting engagements.Make your invitation specific as to the nature of the party, the dress and the time.

Keep the number to a maximum of eight, the ideal quantity for socializing and seating comfortably no matter how large your home is. Today's relaxed lifestyles favour intimate dining — big impersonal cocktail parties are out. Remember that guests with different professions and interests will ensure lively conversation, but don't make the group too disparate.

Once you have selected the menu, make a detailed grocery and wine list. Buy all the non-perishables well ahead of time but leave fresh products such as seafood, vegetables and fruit until the day or two before. Order special cuts of meat or fish well in advance.

Do a "dry run" of your dinner presentation to check supplies of china, cutlery, linen, etc. and to decide which serving plates to use for which dish. A co-ordinated colour scheme is important. Make sure the tones of tablecloth, napkins and flowers are complementary both to each other and to the colours of the food. The type of food will influence your choice of platter — an earthy peasant dish, for example, would look better on stoneware than on fine china. Make sure you have enough candles, fuel for chafing dishes and any specialty items such as punch bowls and warming trays. The latter may be rented if necessary,along with a large coffee urn. Arrange for flowers in advance, telling the florist the mood of the occasion and the colour scheme.

For a buffet, plan exactly where each food dish will go. Dinner plates should be put on one end of the table or counter and napkins and cutlery at the opposite end to pick up last. Locate wine at a separate table or serve guests individually when they are seated. (Most of the buffet foods in this book require only a fork, an advantage which eliminates tricky balancing acts for your guests.)

Timing is essential to the success of any event but advance preparation and planning, as suggested throughout this book, will ensure that on the day of your party everything is under control. Allow the morning for tidying up the house (don't fuss too much, your guests are not coming on a house inspection) and to check last minute details. I make sure I get in my daily five-mile jog, then relax in a leisurely bath so I am at my best to greet my guests.

Generally, I serve cocktails from 7.30 to 8.30 pm; this allows time for late arrivals. When everyone is relaxed and sociable I start heating the first and main courses. Allow for two pre-dinner drinks and one to two appetizers per person. Any more will ruin their appetite for the delights to come. Allow 30 minutes between courses at a sit-down dinner for full appreciation of the food and the company. By 10, it's usually time for dessert and coffee in the living room but if conversation is lively and guests relaxed there's no need to rush them away. You might even choose to serve the remainder of the meal, including liqueurs, at the table. Let the mood of the evening, not etiquette, dictate such things.

At a buffet, put out all the main course dishes first. Then, when every-one has stopped going back for seconds, clear the table completely and bring out the dessert and coffee. This is where a giant urn is helpful — guests can easily help themselves. Liqueurs can be served at the same table as the wine. One very firm rule in my house is not to let the guests help to clear away the dishes. This practice tends to break up the party. If you have older children, ask them to help you.

When calculating wine needs, allow half a bottle per person, with another two or more bottles in reserve. Is there a "proper" wine to serve with individual foods? The answer is "no." Serve what tastes best to you. Generally though, delicate meats such as veal, chicken or fish go well with white wines and robust red meats with full-bodied reds. White wine should be chilled and chilling also often improves light fruity reds. Overchilling may mask the flavour — thirty minutes to an hour in the refrigerator is usually ample. If you forget to chill, place the bottles in a bucket filled with ice and water for 15 minutes, then turn bottles upside down to chill the necks a few minutes before serving.

It's a myth that red wine needs to be opened 30 minutes ahead of time in order to breathe. This could in fact cause a good old wine to lose some flavour. Open the wine just before pouring. It will develop its full character quickly in the glass because a much larger surface area is exposed to the air. If the cork breaks, reinsert the corkscrew to remove remaining cork, then filter wine through cheesecloth or coffee filter. Leftover wine should be recorked immediately, stored in the refrigerator and used as quickly as possible. If it starts to go stale, use it to cook with.

If red wine spills on your carpet, simply smother it with salt or baking soda, leave on overnight then vacuum. This works most of the time. If in doubt, call your rug dealer.

It's not chic to pop a champagne cork loudly. Here's how to open and serve this most elegant of wines properly: First, wipe off the chilled bottle. Take off the wire mesh around the cork and hold the bottle in one hand, slightly tilted and pointed away from your body. With the other hand, grasp the cork firmly. Rotate the bottle slowly and pull it downwards so the gases are gently released. To pour, hold the bottle with your thumb in the bottom identation and support the bottle with your fingers. Fill each glass one-third full, then, when the bubbles have subsided, add a further third — but no more.

Family Gathering

Shrimp Mousse
Stuffed Cherry Tomatoes
Stuffed Mushrooms
Olive Martini Loaf
Crown Roast of Pork with Spiced Apple Sauce
Carrots au Gratin
Baked Mushrooms Deluxe
Cauliflower and Broccoli Medley
Frozen Grand Marnier Souffle
Rum Cake de Maison
White Riesling and Red or White Bordeaux wines

For that very special occasion when relatives gather for a joyous reunion a crown roast of pork adds panache. This elegant menu will easily serve 14 and can be served as a formal sit-down dinner or buffet style. Everything that requires much work can be done ahead of time and the crown roast, while it looks spectacular, needs little attention and carves beautifully. This menu would make a pleasant change for a Thanksgiving or Easter dinner.

Shrimp Mousse

This serves equally well as appetizer or salad course. In addition, it makes an ideal light luncheon.   Serves 15

3 cups small shrimp, coarsely chopped (750 mL)
8 tablespoons finely chopped celery (125 mL)
2 tablespoons lemon juice (30 mL)
1 teaspoon Dijon mustard (5 mL)
salt and pepper
2 envelopes unflavoured gelatin
½ cup cold water (125 mL)
2 tablespoons white wine or vermouth (30 mL)
1 cup cream, whipped (250 mL)
2 cups mayonnaise (500 mL)

In a bowl combine shrimp, celery, lemon juice, mustard, salt and pepper. Set aside. In a small saucepan, soften gelatin in cold water and dissolve over low heat until melted. Add wine, cool slightly, then fold in whipped cream, mayonnaise and shrimp mixture. Oil one 6-cup (1.5 L) ring or fish mould and pour in the mousse. Chill overnight. Unmould on a bed of butter lettuce and garnish with cherry tomatoes, shrimps and ripe olives. Serve with crackers.

Stuffed Cherry Tomatoes

These tasty tomato morsels add colour and variety to any appetizer tray. Allow two per person. Serves 12.

24 cherry tomatoes
8 to 10 ounces cream cheese at room temperature (250 to 300 g)
1 tablespoon chopped green onion (15 mL)
½ teaspoon dill (2 mL)
2 tablespoons finely chopped toasted pecans (30 mL)
2 tablespoons light cream (30 mL)
¼ teaspoon Dijon mustard (1 mL)
1 tablespoon lemon juice (15 mL)
baby shrimp or chopped toasted pecans for topping

Wash tomatoes. Cut off the tops and scoop out all the pulp and seeds. Pat insides dry with paper towels. Cream cheese until soft, add onion, dill, pecans, cream, mustard and lemon juice. Divide evenly to fill tomato shells. Decorate with shrimp or pecans. Cover and refrigerate overnight or make them the morning of serving.

Stuffed Mushrooms

An unusual combination of smoked salmon and whipped cream creates a beautifully delicate flavour. Serves 12 to 14.

24 medium-sized mushrooms
lemon juice
¼ pound smoked salmon (125 g)
½ cup whipping cream, whipped (125 mL)
¼ to ½ teaspoon dill weed (1 to 2 mL)
paprika

Remove stems from mushrooms. If they are brown, peel the outer skin; if white, just rub with damp paper towel. Sprinkle caps with lemon juice. Finely chop salmon and fold into the whipped cream along with the dill. Spoon mixture onto mushroom caps, sprinkle lightly with paprika and chill. These can be made the morning of serving.

Olive Martini Loaf

Nippy and crunchy, this bread contains gin, vodka or vermouth, along with sour olives. Tuck an extra loaf into the freezer for emergencies. Makes 16 to 20 thin slices.

2⅔ cups all-purpose flour (650 mL)
1 tablespoon baking powder (15 mL)
pinch salt
2 tablespoons sugar (30 mL)
5 tablespoons butter (75 mL)
1 large egg
¼ cup liquid from olives (50 mL)
1 cup milk (250 mL)
¼ cup gin, vodka or vermouth (50 mL)
¼ cup Parmesan cheese (50 mL)
½ cup finely chopped walnuts (125 mL)
1 cup pimiento-stuffed olives, drained (250 mL)

Blend flour, baking powder, salt and sugar in mixing bowl. Cut in the butter and blend well. In a separate bowl, beat egg, olive liquid, milk, liquor and cheese, add to the flour mixture and gently blend together. Fold in nuts and whole olives. Turn into well-greased 9 by 5-inch (22 by 12 cm) loaf pan and bake at 350°F (180°C) for about 45 to 55 minutes or until it tests done. Cool. It will keep fresh for two days and freezes well. Serve thinly sliced with butter.

Crown Roast of Pork

A regal banquet made colourfully complete with cranberry apple stuffing and spiced apple sauce. Order the roast from your butcher well ahead of time.   Serves 12 to 14.

Crown roast of pork
salt
ground sage
cranberry-apple stuffing
1 12-ounce jar apricot preserves, melted (340 mL)
cherry tomatoes or kumquats to decorate ribs
watercress for garnish

Order two half-loin crowns of pork with ten to twelve ribs on each loin. This will allow 1 to 1½ chops per person. Have the butcher remove all excess fat on the inside and the outside. About six hours before serving, place pork in a large shallow roasting pan with a rack, rib sides up. Line the inside of the crown with a double layer of foil to prevent the stuffing from falling out. Sprinkle entire roast with salt and sage, spoon stuffing into the centre and refrigerate until ready to roast.

   Pre-heat oven to 325°F (160°C). About 4½ hours before serving, cover the entire centre of the stuffed crown as well as the ribs with foil and roast in oven for three hours. Remove foil. Peel and core one apple, slice thinly and arrange in concentric circles over the stuffing. Brush side and ribs of the roast with drippings and bake for a further 40 minutes. Brush surfaces again and bake for another 30 minutes. Total cooking time: 4 hours, 10 minutes. Remove to a platter and top each rib with tomato or kumquat. Carve from the top down, between the ribs, allowing one rib per person. Spoon stuffing onto each plate. Serve with hot spiced applesauce.

Cranberry-Apple Stuffing

½ cup butter (125 mL)
1 small onion, chopped
½ teaspoon salt (2 mL)
½ teaspoon poultry seasoning (2 mL)
pinch pepper
1 cup finely chopped celery (250 mL)
4 cups (1 L) day-old bread in ⅓-inch (1 cm) cubes
3 tablespoons water (45 mL)
2 cups pared and sliced green apples (500 mL)
lemon juice
1½ cups fresh or frozen cranberries, chopped (375 mL)

Melt butter in large skillet and saute onion until slightly tender. Add salt, seasoning, pepper and celery, saute briefly, then add bread cubes and toss. Add water, toss to blend. Cover and refrigerate overnight. The next morning, dip apple slices in lemon juice and add to bread mixture along with cranberries.

Spiced Applesauce

2 14-ounce (398 mL) cans applesauce (or make your own)
3 tablespoons brown sugar (45 mL)
2 teaspoons lemon juice (10 mL)
½ teaspoon nutmeg (2 mL)
2 teaspoons cinnamon (10 mL)

Mix all together and refrigerate until needed. Heat gently to serve.

Carrots au Gratin

Celery soup gives the carrots a slight nut-like flavour. This dish is great for a crowd. It's a family favourite from sister-in-law Dianne — a tradition with our Christmas turkey.   Serves 12 to 14.

8 ounces cream cheese (250 g)
1 10-ounce can cream of celery soup (284 mL)
½ cup milk (125 mL)
salt and pepper

3 pounds carrots (1.5 kg)
1 cup bread crumbs (250 mL)
4 tablespoons melted butter (60 mL)
½ cup medium Cheddar cheese, grated (125 mL)

Butter a shallow 1½ (1.5 L) quart casserole. Combine cream cheese, soup, milk, salt and pepper in a blender or food processor until blended. Grate carrots and add to cream cheese mixture, mix well and pour into casserole. Mix bread crumbs, melted butter and Cheddar and sprinkle over the top. Cover and refrigerate overnight. Bake uncovered at 325°F (160°C) along with the pork roast for about 45 to 50 minutes or until golden and hot. If the topping becomes too brown, cover it with tin foil.

Baked Mushrooms Deluxe

A very rich and creamy dish to complement roasts, chicken or steak. Make it the day ahead.   Serves 12 to 14.

3¾ pounds fresh mushrooms, medium size, unsliced (1.75 kg)
4 tablespoons finely chopped green onions (60 mL)
1¼ cup butter (300 mL)
juice of ½ lemon
4 tablespoons finely chopped parsley (60 mL)
¾ teaspoon Hungarian sweet paprika (3 mL)
1¼ cup flour (300 mL)
3 cups chicken broth (750 mL)
¾ cup sour cream (200 mL)
salt and pepper
½ to ¾ cup cracker crumbs (125 to 200 mL)

Saute mushrooms and onions lightly in half the butter. Sprinkle with lemon juice, parsley and paprika. Remove to shallow 2-quart (2 L) casserole. To the butter and juices in the skillet, add remaining butter and blend in the flour to make a paste. Add chicken broth slowly to make a sauce. Add sour cream, salt and pepper, pour over the mushrooms and blend well. Sauce will be thick but will thin out during baking. Cover and refrigerate overnight. Bake at 325°F (160°C) for about 45 minutes or until hot and bubbly.

Cauliflower and Broccoli Medley

Crisp and colourful, with a Chinese touch.   Serves 12 to 14

> 2 pounds broccoli (1 kg)
> 2 medium cauliflowers
> 1 clove garlic, crushed
> ½ tablespoon minced preserved or green ginger (7 mL)
> 4 tablespoons peanut oil (60 mL)
> 10 tablespoons water (150 mL)
> 1½ tablespoons soy sauce (25 mL)
> lemon juice

Separate broccoli and cauliflower tops from stems and divide into flowerets. In a large frying pan, saute the ginger and garlic in the oil until lightly browned. Add vegetables, stir and toss, then add water and soy sauce. Cover and steam for about 4 minutes, or until barely tender. You can refrigerate them at this stage. About five minutes before serving, add a little more water to the pan and steam until hot. Add a good sprinkling of lemon juice and serve.

Rum Cake de Maison

Don't turn the page when you see this cake recipe. It may look involved but it should be made the day ahead of serving and is well worth the effort for a special anniversary, birthday or family gathering.   Serves 18

> 2 cups sifted white flour (500 mL)
> 2 teaspoons baking powder (10 mL)
> pinch salt
> ¼ teaspoon baking soda (1 mL)
> ½ cup butter (125 mL)
> 1 cup white sugar (250 mL)
>
> 2 eggs, separated
> 1 teaspoon grated orange rind (5 mL)
> ½ cup orange juice (125 mL)
> 3 tablespoons white rum (45 mL)
> ¼ teaspoon almond extract (1 mL)
> ¼ teaspoon vanilla (1 mL)

Grease two 9-inch (22 cm) layer cake pans and cover the bottoms with waxed paper, cut to fit. Heat oven to 350°F (180°C). In a bowl, mix flour, baking powder, salt and baking soda. In another bowl with electric mixer beat butter until soft and creamy; gradually add ¾ cup (200 mL) sugar and continue beating until light and fluffy. Add egg yolks, one at a time, then the orange rind. Combine orange juice, rum and flavourings and blend with egg yolk mixture. Gradually add flour mixture, beating at low speed.

In a medium bowl, beat egg whites to soft peaks, gradually blend in the remaining ¼ cup (50 mL) sugar and continue beating until stiff peaks form. Fold egg whites gently into batter, then pour into the prepared pans. Bake for about 25 minutes or until tops spring back when lightly pressed. (They will not rise very high.) Cool in pans on wire racks for ten minutes, then remove. Cool, then refrigerate or freeze. If you freeze the cakes, take them out to thaw two days before assembly.

Split cake layers in two and sprinkle each layer with 4 tablespoons (60 mL) rum. Spread whipped cream filling between layers and ice top with chocolate icing. Decorate with chocolate coffee beans or chocolate curls.

Whipped Cream Filling

    2 teaspoons unflavoured gelatin (10 mL)
    2 tablespoons cold water (30 mL)
    ⅓ cup white rum (75 mL)
    1 pint whipping cream (500 mL)
    ½ cup icing sugar (125 mL)

In a small saucepan, combine gelatin and water and heat over low flame until dissolved. Add rum and set aside to cool. Combine cream and icing sugar and beat until thick. Gradually blend in the cooled gelatin mixture with spatula. Refrigerate until needed.

Chocolate Icing

    4 squares unsweetened chocolate
    1 cup icing sugar (250 mL)
    2 tablespoons hot water (30 mL)
    2 large eggs
    6 tablespoons soft butter (90 mL)

In a double boiler over hot not boiling water melt the chocolate. Remove from heat and with a large spoon or beater gradually beat in icing sugar and water. Then beat in eggs, one at a time, the butter, 2 tablespoons (30 mL) at a time and continue to beat until smooth. Spread while still warm.

The cake should be taken from the refrigerator about 30 minutes before serving to allow the icing to soften for easier cutting.

Frozen Grand Marnier Souffle

I could have devoured the whole souffle myself when my friend Liz Bryan served it to us and I couldn't resist asking for the recipe. It's great by itself or with fresh strawberies or raspberries.

> *2 large oranges*
> *2 large lemons*
> *1½ tablespoons gelatin (25 mL)*
> *9 egg yolks*
> *1¾ cup sugar (450 mL)*
> *3 egg whites*
> *1½ cups milk (375 mL)*
> *½ cup Grand Marnier (125 mL)*
> *2 cups whipping cream (500 mL)*

Grate rind from oranges and lemons and reserve. Squeeze juice; there should be 1 cup (250 mL). Sprinkle gelatin over juice to soften. Beat egg yolks with sugar until mixture ribbons. Scald milk and add to yolks in a steady stream, stirring constantly. Transfer to heavy saucepan or double boiler and cook, stirring with wooden spoon, until custard is thick and coats spoon. Do not boil. Add gelatin mixture and stir until dissolved. Strain custard, add rind and Grand Marnier, put saucepan in bowl of crushed ice and stir until completely cool and thick but not set. Beat egg whites until stiff. In separate bowl, beat cream until thick. Fold two together, then fold very gently into the cold custard. Turn into souffle dish and freeze for at least 6 hours.

Theatrical Special

Dubonnet or Chateau de Beaulon Pineau des Charentes
French Pizza Dianne
Wine Cheeses with Crackers and Fruit
Hearts of Palm Salad
Shrimp Thermidor in Croustade
Asparagus Spears
Frozen Banana Meringue with Chocolate Sauce
Wines: Dry white Bordeaux or white Burgundy

How do you plan a dinner party around an 8:30 curtain call? Just choose a menu like this one. It is prepared totally in advance and is easy to serve, yet it looks impressive and tastes sumptuous, but remember not to linger too long over the appetizers.

This menu is also good for other occasions when time and effort are in short supply. It has become a Christmas Eve tradition for my family and friends. After a hectic day of last minute shopping and gift-wrapping, everyone — including the cook — relaxes around the Christmas tree to enjoy the festive atmosphere — and the good food!

Aperitif

The ruby Pineau des Charentes is my favourite French aperitif, somewhat similar in flavour to red Dubonnet. Purists like to drink it straight but I prefer to serve it on ice with a twist of lemon. It is made from grape juice with cognac added and should be served in tiny doses for it is rich and smooth. It is expensive but worth the splurge for a special occasion.

Wine Cheeses and Fruit

Arrange a few assorted wine cheeses on a platter with wedges of pear, apple and a few clusters of grapes. These will whet the appetite nicely.

French Pizza Dianne

This is a lifesaver that you can whisk out of the freezer for a quick appetizer, late night snack or even a light meal. My sister-in-law Dianne always manages to come up with something special for me whenever I fly in to Toronto and her special pizza hits the spot.

Makes about 20 slices

1 package frozen puff pastry
1 egg yolk blended with 1 teaspoon water
½ cup spaghetti sauce, canned or your own (125 mL)
20 thin slices pepperoni
5 slices ham, 4 inches square (10 cm²), ¼-inch (6 mm) thick
3 tablespoons chopped green onions (45 mL)
pinch Italian seasoning
6 ounces Mozzarella cheese, grated (300 g)

Thaw puff pastry and roll into a 9 x 16 inch (22 x 45 cm) rectangle. Cut into two pieces, one four inches (10 cm) and one five inches (12 cm) in width. Brush edges with egg yolk mixture. Place larger rectangle on a greased cookie sheet and spread spaghetti sauce over to within one inch of the edges. Arrange pepperoni, ham, onions and seasoning on top, then sprinkle over the cheese. Place the other piece of dough on top and seal with the bottom crust. Press edges together with a fork. Brush top with egg yolk mixture and make four slits in the top. Bake at 425°F (220°C) for about 25 minutes, cut into two-inch (5 cm) squares and serve hot.

For future use, cool, wrap and freeze uncooked pizza, then heat at 350°F (180°C) for about 30 minutes to serve. Whenever I have leftover spaghetti sauce I make two or three of these pizzas to tuck in the freezer. And if you don't have ham or pepperoni on hand, use green peppers, roast beef, chicken or other remnants. It's always good.

Hearts of Palm Salad

The hearts or tender shoots of the palm tree add a unique flavour to any salad. They can be found in cans at most specialty food sections. Be sure to give them a try. Serves 8 well.

    2 to 3 heads iceberg or butter lettuce
    1 14-ounce can hearts of palm, drained (398 mL)
    3 tablespoons pimento, chopped (45 mL)
    2 avocados, cubed

Just before serving, tear the lettuce into bite-sized bits and combine in a salad bowl with avocado, pimento and hearts of palm, sliced 1/4-inch (6 mm) thick. Pour over only enough dressing to coat the greens.

Dressing
    3/4 cup salad oil, olive oil, or combination (200 mL)
    1/4 cup white wine vinegar (50 mL)
    1/4 teaspoon Dijon mustard (1 mL)
    salt, pepper
    generous squeeze of lemon juice

Combine and shake well. This can be made up a few days ahead of serving and refrigerated.

Shrimp Thermidor in Croustade

Really a glorified, elegant sandwich, this dish is similar to the classic Lobster Thermidor but it is served in a croustade — a lightly-browned bread shell. It is a quick recipe, a little like a fondue, but it looks impressive. The bread shell and the shrimp filling can be prepared the day ahead. Assemble and reheat minutes before serving.   Serves 6.

Croustade
With a bread knife, trim all crusts from two 1 pound (500 g) loaves of unsliced bread, making the tops of the loaves flat and even like the sides. (Bread can be white or whole wheat.) Carefully hollow out each loaf, leaving a one-inch (2.5 cm) shell. Cut off one side from each bread shell, then fit the three-sided shells together to make one large shell, and secure with toothpicks. Wrap well in plastic. Set aside ½ cup (125 mL) butter to be melted for the last minute assembly.

Shrimp Filling
⅓ *cup butter (75 mL)*
¾ *cup flour (200 mL)*
¼ *teaspoon salt (1 mL)*
dash pepper
1 cup light cream (250 mL)
1 cup dry white wine (250 mL)
2 cups medium Cheddar cheese, grated (500 mL)
1¼ pounds cooked baby shrimp (625 g)
1½ cups tomatoes, peeled and cubed (750 mL)
parsley sprigs for garnish

Make the thermidor sauce: Over low heat in a medium saucepan melt butter and blend in flour, salt and pepper, mixing until smooth. Gradually add the light cream and wine and bring to a boil, stirring constantly. Reduce heat and simmer for one minute. Gradually add grated cheese, stirring after each addition until all is melted. Cover and refrigerate overnight.

On the day of serving: Add shrimp to sauce, mixing well. Place in casserole dish and heat in a 350°F (180°C) oven for about 30 minutes or until hot. Add tomatoes a few minutes before serving and let them heat

Making the Croustade: Hollow out two loaves of bread, slice off the sides and fasten together with toothpicks. Bread shell is then brushed with melted butter and baked.

through. (The sauce may also be heated on top of the stove, provided it is constantly stirred.) While the shrimp is heating, place bread shell on an ungreased cookie sheet and brush the entire loaf with melted butter. Bake at 350°F (180°C) until golden brown, about 30 minutes. Keep warm until shrimp is hot. Spoon hot filling into the croustade and garnish with parsley. To serve, slice crosswise into one-inch servings and spoon the shrimp mixture over.

(Depending on the amount of juice in the shrimp or the tomatoes you might need to adjust the thickness of the filling — blend in more wine or more flour.)

Frozen Banana Meringue with Chocolate Sauce

This refreshing blend of bananas, meringue and out-of-this-world choc-olate sauce also comes from sister-in-law Dianne in Toronto. It can be made and frozen weeks ahead of serving and the chocolate sauce can be made a week before and stored in the refrigerator. In summer you can vary this recipe by serving it with a strawberry sauce. Serves 8.

Meringue
   3 egg whites
   ¾ cup white sugar (berry sugar is best) (200 mL)
   ½ teaspoon vanilla (2 mL)
   ¼ teaspoon white vinegar (1 mL)

Beat egg whites until stiff. Gradually beat in the sugar, a tablespoon at a time, then add vanilla and vinegar. Cut two pieces of wax paper five inches (12 cm) by eight inches (20 cm) and place on a cookie sheet. Divide the meringue mixture equally and spread over the two pieces of wax paper to make two even layers. Bake at 275°F (140°C) for 45 to 55 minutes or until firm. Remove wax paper immediately, cool then store uncovered in a cupboard until filling is ready.

Filling
   1 cup mashed ripe bananas (250 mL)
   pinch salt
   1 tablespoon fresh lemon juice (15 mL)
   ½ pint whipping cream (250 mL)
   ¼ cup icing sugar (50 mL)

Combine bananas, salt and lemon juice. Whip cream with icing sugar until fluffy and thick and fold into the banana mixture.
   Spread banana mixture evenly on one meringue layer, top with second layer, wrap well and freeze. Remove from freezer about 25 minutes before serving to let it soften, cut into slices and pour chocolate sauce over.

Chocolate Sauce

This sauce is exquisite. It is great for Pears Helene or over just plain vanilla ice cream. It will keep for about a week in the refrigerator, but if you have chocolate lovers in your family, just watch it disappear! I usually make double quantities in self defence.   Makes ¾ cup (200 mL)

> 4 ounces semi-sweet chocolate (125 g)
> 2 tablespoons butter (30 mL)
> ¼ cup white or golden corn syrup (50 mL)
> ⅓ cup Kahlua or Tia Maria (75 mL)
> ¼ cup whipping cream (50 mL)

Combine all ingredients in a double boiler. When chocolate has melted, simmer for about 20 minutes longer. Put into sealed container and refrigerate. To serve: reheat until softened in double boiler and stir until smooth and fluid.

For Pears Helene, place pear halves in individual sherbert dishes, add scoops of vanilla ice cream and top with chocolate sauce. Add whipped cream garnish if desired.

A Christmas Feast

Frozen Rum Daiquiri
Quiche Lorraine Tartlets
Olive Cheese Puffs
Roast Suckling Pig with Pork Stuffing
Potatoes Romanoff
Pecan-Orange Sweet Potatoes
Fiddlehead Ferns
Crunchy Granola Bread
Charlotte Chantilly with Raspberry Sauce
Chocolate Chip Cookies

This Christmas dinner is a departure from traditional turkey. Its roast suckling pig, complete with apple in its mouth, is reminiscent of the medieval wassailing feasts of jolly old England but its vegetable accompaniments are far from old-fashioned — fiddlehead ferns and orange pecan sweet potatoes. The bread is a crunchy granola braid, the dessert a spectacular Charlotte Chantilly in a pool of raspberry sauce.

Frozen Rum Daiquiri

This is an excellent recipe for a crowd because it dispenses with the need for a bar-tender. It can be frozen weeks ahead and will refreeze if any is left, which is doubtful. Extremely refreshing, it is light and won't spoil the appetite. I usually keep a batch or two in my freezer for holiday and summer entertaining. Serves 6 for pre-dinner drinks.

1 bottle white rum
1 12½-ounce tin frozen limeade (355 mL)
1 large bottle 7-Up
¾ cup of water (200 mL)

Combine all ingredients and freeze in airtight container. Twenty minutes before serving, transfer to a punch bowl and stir until smooth and mushy. Pour into small goblets. Garnish with slice of lime and a stemmed cherry.

Quiche Lorraine Tartlets

Pastry par excellence to serve with cocktails — they just melt in the mouth. The tartlets freeze beautifully — just reheat an extra 10 minutes. Double the filling and you have the makings of a traditional quiche cooked in an 8 or 9-inch (20 or 22 *pie* shell.

Pastry
>½ cup shortening)
>1⅓ cup all purpose flour (325 mL)
>2½ table... ice water (40 mL)

Filling
>6 slices of bacon
>2 ounces Swiss cheese (65 g)
>2 eggs
>1 cup whipping cream (250 mL) — 2% okay
>½ teaspoon salt (2 mL)
>pinch nutmeg
>1 teaspoon sugar (5 mL)
>dash of pepper

To make pastry: in medium bowl cut shortening into flour until mixture resembles small peas. Sprinkle ice water over mixture, a tablespoon (15 mL) at a time, tossing with fork until all particles are moistened. Form into a ball. Roll out ¼-inch (6 mm) thick on a lightly-floured surface and cut into 3-inch (7.5 cm) circles. Fit each circle into 24 small muffin pans (1¾ inch (4.5 cm) cups).

To make the filling: Heat oven to 400°F (200°C). Fry bacon till crisp and crumble. Shred cheese. Combine eggs, cream, salt, nutmeg, sugar and pepper and beat to blend well. Sprinkle each tart shell with bacon, then cheese. Fill each cup ¾ full with egg mixture and sprinkle tops with nutmeg. Bake for 10 minutes or until pastry is golden, then reduce heat to 350°F (180°C) and bake for 10 minutes longer. Don't overbake. Cool, remove from pans, freeze or store in refrigerator. Reheat for 10 minutes at 325°F (160°C) until heated through.

Olive Cheese Puffs

These are old standbys that add to any appetizer tray. They freeze well. Cocktail onions, gherkins or pickles may be used instead of olives.

Makes 24.

1 cup sharp Cheddar cheese (250 mL)
¼ cup soft butter (50 mL)
½ cup flour (125 mL)
¼ teaspoon salt (1 mL)
½ teaspoon paprika (2 mL)
24 stuffed green olives

Blend cheese and butter and stir in flour, salt and paprika. Mould about one teaspoon (5 mL) of dough around each olive, covering it completely. Bake in 400°F (200°C) oven for about 10 minutes until golden. To serve, reheat at 325°F (160°C) for five minutes or until hot.

Roast Stuffed Suckling Pig

A suckling pig makes any occasion memorable. It creates a stunning centrepiece for a buffet decorated with festive garlands of cranberries. Be sure to order your pig well in advance.

Serves 12.

1 12 to 15-pound suckling pig (6 to 7 kg)
1 ½ teaspoons salt (7 mL)
¼ teaspoon black pepper (1 mL)
¼ teaspoon ground ginger (1 mL)
3 tablespoons butter, melted (45 mL)
2 cups boiling water (500 mL)
1 onion, chopped
1 carrot
1 stick celery
1 small apple
2 cherries
cranberries
Rice and Pork Stuffing

Wash pig under running water, drain and wipe dry with paper towels. If the pig is frozen, thaw in refrigerator the day previous. Mix salt, pepper and ginger and rub the inside of the pig. Fill cavity loosely with stuffing, close opening with skewers and lace tightly with string. Wipe skin and rub with melted butter. Put a small block in pig's mouth to brace it for the apple which you insert after it is cooked. Slash skin a few times to release fat during roasting. Tuck legs under and place pig on a rack in large shallow pan. Pour boiling water into pan and add onion, carrot and celery. Cover pig with foil and roast in preheated 325°F (160°C) oven for 5 to 6 hours, basting every 45 minutes with the water. Add more water if needed. When very tender remove to a platter. Put apple in mouth and cherries in eye sockets, and garland with threaded cranberries. Rub entire pig with melted butter until it shines. (If pig is too big to fit in your oven, simply cut out a section from the middle and sew ends together. You can later disguise the seam with cranberries. Cook cut-out section alongside.)

Rice and Pork Stuffing

    1 pound lean pork sausage meat (500 g)
    1 onion, chopped
    1 cup sliced mushrooms (250 mL)
    1 tablespoon chopped parsley (15 mL)
    2 tablespoons flour (30 mL)
    2 tablespoons butter (30 mL)
    1 teaspoon salt (5 mL)
    ¼ teaspoon pepper (1 mL)
    2 teaspoons poultry seasoning (10 mL)
    2 tablespoons sherry (30 mL)
    4 cups cooked rice (1 L)
    2 tablespoons chopped celery leaves (30 mL)

Cook meat, drain off fat. Saute onion and mushrooms until limp, add parsley and flour-and-butter mixed, and stir until thickened. Season with salt, pepper and seasoning, add sherry and cook for a few minutes. Add cooked sausage meat, rice and celery leaves. Cool, then spoon into pig cavity.

Potatoes Romanoff

An old favourite potato casserole, this goes well with almost any meat or poultry. It can be made the day ahead.   Serves 8.

  6 large potatoes
  2 green onions, finely chopped
  ½ teaspoon salt (2 mL)
  pinch pepper
  ¾ cup Cheddar cheese, grated (200 mL)
  1 pint sour cream (500 mL)

Peel and cook potatoes just until tender. Cool and grate into large bowl. Add green onion, salt, pepper and cheese and fold in sour cream. Put into an 8½ by 11-inch (20 x 30 cm) casserole and cover with more cheese. Bake at 350°F (180°C) for 35 to 40 minutes or until golden and hot.

Pecan-Orange Sweet Potatoes

Everyone loves this vegetable dish. The contrast of the tart orange sauce with the sweet potatoes is temptingly tangy. It's great with turkey. This can be made the day ahead and can also be frozen.   Serves 8.

  8 medium sized sweet potatoes, cooked
  2 oranges, peeled and thinly sliced
  2½ tablespoons cornstarch (35 mL)
  1 cup brown sugar (225 mL)
  ½ teaspoon salt (2 mL)
  2 tablespoons grated orange rind (30 mL)
  ¼ cup butter (50 mL)
  2 cups orange juice (500 mL)
  ½ cup pecan halves (125 mL)

Peel and slice potatoes into 1-inch (2.5 cm) slices. Arrange alternate layers of potato and orange slices in 1½ quart (1.5 L) casserole. Combine cornstarch, brown sugar, and salt, add orange peel and butter, then pour in orange juice and cook over low heat, stirring, until smooth and thick. Pour sauce over potatoes and oranges and top with pecans. Bake in 350°F (180°C) oven for about 30 minutes or until heated and glazed.

Crunchy Granola Bread

Great with a hearty bowl of soup and an assortment of cheeses, this bread is quick to make as it needs only one rising. It freezes well. Makes two loaves.

2 teaspoons sugar (10 mL)
2 envelopes (2 tablespoons) dried yeast (30 mL)
1 cup warm water (250 mL)
1 cup scalded milk (250 mL)
½ cup cold water (125 mL)
¼ cup oil (50 mL)
¼ cup honey, molasses or brown sugar (50 mL)
2½ teaspoons salt (12 mL)
5 cups (approx.) all purpose flour (1.25 L)
2 cups whole wheat flour (500 mL)
1½ cups crunchy granola (375 mL)

Dissolve sugar and yeast in warm water. Put scalded milk into a large bowl and add next four ingredients. Beat in 2 cups (500 mL) white flour, then the yeast. Add whole wheat flour and beat to mix. Add more white flour to make soft dough. Knead until smooth. Knead granola in and add more white flour if needed to make stiff and sticky dough. Form into flat ball, cut into 6 wedges, tuck in pointed ends and roll and twist to make six 9-inch (22 cm) long ropes. Braid three at a time to form 2 loaves. Cover with wet towel and leave rise until double, about 1¼ hours. Bake at 375°F (190°C) about 35 or 40 minutes or until golden brown.

Charlotte Chantilly
with Raspberry Sauce

This is definitely numero uno! It is one of the most sensuous of desserts, sheer ambrosia. A regal mould of creamy white sits in a rich red pool of raspberries.

Serves 12

¾ cup white sugar (200 mL)
⅓ cup water (75 mL)
3 egg yolks
dash salt
1 cup crumbled almond macaroon cookies (250 mL)
8 to 10 ladyfingers
4 tablespoons (or more) Grand Marnier, white rum or sherry (60 mL)
1 pint whipping cream (500 mL)
2 teaspoons vanilla (10 mL)
½ teaspoon almond extract (2 mL)

Line a 6 to 8-inch (15 to 22 cm) mould or souffle dish with foil. In a small saucepan combine the sugar and water and bring to a boil over medium heat, stirring until sugar is dissolved. Boil gently without stirring to 230°F (110°C) on a candy thermometre or until a little of the sugar mixture spins a thread when dropped from a spoon. In a medium bowl, with mixer at medium speed, beat yolks and salt until light. Gradually beat in the hot syrup in a thin stream, continuing to beat until mixture begins to cool — about 2 minutes. Stir in the macaroons and refrigerate for 10 minutes. Sprinkle ladyfingers with liquor. Combine cream with flavourings and beat until stiff. Fold whipped cream into macaroon mixture. Turn half the mixture into the prepared mould. Make a layer with lady fingers and pour in the remaining mixture. Freeze. (It will keep for weeks.) Unmould and serve on a rimmed cake plate, spoon raspberry sauce around the base and decorate top with additional whipped cream and chocolate curls.

Raspberry Sauce

2 packages frozen raspberries, thawed
2 tablespoons cornstarch (30 mL)
½ cup red currant jelly (125 mL)

Drain raspberries, reserving liquid. There should be enough liquid to make 2 cups. In a small saucepan blend the liquid with cornstarch and bring to boil, stirring constantly. Continue to boil for 5 minutes until thickened. Stir in jelly until melted. Remove from heat, add raspberries. Refrigerate, covered, until cold. This can be made the day ahead.

Toasted Oatmeal Chocolate Chip Cookies

Everyone has a recipe for chocolate chip cookies but the secret of this one is the oatmeal: it's toasted in the butter before baking. This makes the cookies crisp and nutty — they are positively the best you've ever eaten.

Makes 2½ dozen.

¾ cup butter (200 mL)
2½ cups oatmeal (not instant, not large flake) (625 mL)
½ cup flour (125 mL)
1 teaspoon cinnamon (5mL)
¼ teaspoon salt (1 mL)
½ teaspoon baking soda (2 mL)
1 cup brown sugar (250 mL)
1 egg
1 teaspoon vanilla (5 mL)
1½ cups chocolate chips (375 mL)

Melt butter in electric frypan set at 325°F (160°C) and heat until butter is light brown. Do not burn. Add oats and stir constantly until oats are golden and toasted. Remove from heat and cool thoroughly. In mixing bowl combine egg, sugar and vanilla and beat until light. Sift flour with cinnamon, salt and soda and add to egg mixture, along with the oatmeal. Add chocolate chips. Drop by teaspoon onto greased baking sheet and bake at 350°F (180°C) for 8 to 10 minutes or until golden.

A Morning Affair

Kir
Country Terrine or Pâté
Baguette Bread
Salad Nicoise
or
Vegetable Melange Salad (page 75)
Seafood or Mushroom Pie a La Varenne
Kahlua Mousse in Chocolate Cups
Strawberries and Pineapple Grand Marnier
Champagne or other sparkling wine

Late on a weekend morning is a fresh and lively time for a party and this is why entertaining at brunch or luncheon is so popular. This menu combines my own favourite dishes with some of Anne Willan's specialties from her La Varenne cooking school in Paris. It is typically French in honour of the press reception I hosted for Anne during one of her visits to Vancouver. Starting off with kir, a bubbly French aperitif, and ending with a light mousse, the meal flows smoothly with little effort needed by the hostess. It will be an affair that your guests will long remember.

Kir

Blend six parts of chilled champagne or other sparkling wine with one part of Cassis, the delicious blackcurrant liqueur. If you prefer a stronger blackcurrant flavour, increase the amount of Cassis. This is also good made with a still, medium dry white wine.

Christmas Feast, page
Overleaf: Family Gathering, page 6, photographed at the home of Maurice and Pat Clement, left. Right, Theatrical Special, page 15.

Country Terrine or Pâté

Pâtés are an indispensable part of the French haute cuisine tradition and every French restaurant takes pride in its own version — Pâté Maison. A pâté and a terrine both begin with a mixture of any finely ground meats, liver or game and both are baked. But a terrine is baked in a dish lined with pork or bacon fat and a pâté in a pastry crust. I have experimented with several combinations of ingredients and find this terrine moist and creamy, with a delicate flavour. It should be made two to three days ahead of serving. Makes about 1½ pounds (750 g).

¾ pound bacon (375 g)
½ pound pork loin (250 g)
½ pound boneless veal (250 g)
½ pound chicken livers (250 g)
1 small onion, finely chopped (optional)
1 clove garlic, crushed
2 eggs
¼ cup dry white wine or brandy (50 mL)
¼ cup whipping cream (50 mL)
salt, pepper
1 cup shelled pistachios (optional) (250 mL)
good pinches of thyme, allspice, ground cloves, nutmeg
½ pound baked ham (250 g), ¼ inch (6 mm) thick, cut in strips ¼ inch
   (6 mm) wide

You will need a five-cup (1.25 L) terrine or casserole with a tight-fitting lid. If possible, the terrine should have an air hole so the mixture can be tested with a skewer without removing the lid. Set oven to 350°F (180°C).

Line the terrine or casserole dish with bacon, reserving a few slices for the top. In a food processor, meat grinder or blender grind the pork and veal and set aside. In the same machine, grind the livers. Saute onion in 1 tablespoon (15 mL) of butter until limp and add to the livers along with garlic, eggs, wine, cream, seasonings, nuts and herbs. Mix well. Add ground pork and veal and mix for just a second to blend thoroughly. Spread a third of the meat mixture in the lined terrine, add a layer of half the ham strips and top with another third of the meat. Add the remain-

hearty Soup au Pistou, from Super Soups, page 38.

ing ham slices and top with the rest of the meat. Lay reserved bacon slices on top, cover with a layer of heavy foil, place lid on top and cover with another piece of foil to seal well.

Set the terrine in a roasting pan about half full of boiling water and bake at 350°F (180°C) for 1¾ to 2 hours or until a skewer inserted through the hole in the lid into the centre of the meat for 30 seconds is hot to the touch when withdrawn. If the lid has no hole, lift it to test the terrine. Leave the terrine to cool, weighing down with full cans or other heavy objects; leave in roasting pan in case surplus fat spills over. When cool, remove weights and chill. Serve from the terrine or unmould and glaze with the jellied stock in the bottom of the pan. Slice and serve with French sour gherkins and baguette or regular French bread.

Tightly sealed and stored in the refrigerator, the terrine will keep for up to five days but once cut into, its life is reduced to two days. Pâtés do not freeze well. They absorb too much moisture and lose some of their flavour.

Baguette Bread

Long narrow loaves of freshly-baked baguette bread are part of the French everyday scene — tucked under arms, hanging out of bicycle baskets and adorning every restaurant table. With the long and narrow baguette pans now available in kitchen specialty shops, this traditional bread is now easy to make at home. Unlike most recipes for French bread, this one produces loaves which freeze beautifully although the bread is always best eaten within hours of baking. Any leftovers should be frozen immediately.   Makes 4 loaves.

2 tablespoons sugar (30 mL)	6 cups white flour (1.5 L)
1 tablespoon salt (15 mL)	1 egg white
2½ cups warm water (625 mL)	shortening
1 package dry yeast	

In a large mixing bowl put the sugar, salt, warm water and yeast and stir until dissolved. Mix in most of the flour and beat until it is mixed. Sprinkle the rest of the flour on to the counter, dust hands with flour and knead the bread dough, blending in the remaining flour. Knead for about 10 minutes. If dough is too sticky, add more flour.

Grease the inside of a large bowl with shortening and place dough in it, rolling it over so that it is coated with the grease. (This prevents drying and air crusting during the rising process.) Cover with a damp dish towel and leave to rise in a warm place for about one to 1½ hours until double in bulk.

Punch down and knead several times to remove air. Divide into four equal pieces and shape each into a long rope one inch shorter than the length of the bread pans. Rub bread pans with shortening and lay dough ropes in each, slashing tops diagonally four or five times. Beat egg white slightly and brush over the loaves, painting tops and sides. Raise in a warm place until dough fills the pans, about 1 to 1½ hours. Pre-heat oven to 450°F (230°C) and bake loaves for 15 minutes, then reduce heat to 350°F (180°C) and bake for another 30 minutes until loaves sound hollow when tapped. To give the bread an extra glaze, brush with additional egg white when loaves start their final 30 minutes of baking. Cool on wire racks and serve immediately, or wrap well and freeze. Reheat in a 350°F (180°C) oven for about 10 minutes, well wrapped in foil.

Seafood or Mushroom Pie a La Varenne

Of all the outstanding dishes we prepared at La Varenne, this one is my favourite. It is so versatile — it makes an excellent appetizer, luncheon or light dinner. It is great cooked with mushrooms alone but I like to add fresh shrimp and crabmeat for an added treat. It is lighter than the classic quiche, requiring light cream and egg yolks rather than whipping cream and whole eggs. Make this pie the day before you serve it — its flavour improves. Serves 8 as an appetizer or 4 as a main course.

Pie Pastry

2 cups white flour (500 mL)	2 egg yolks
½ teaspoon salt (2 mL)	4 tablespoons cold water (60 mL)
10 tablespoons butter (150 mL)	1 egg, beaten for the glaze

If using a food processor, combine salt and flour first, then add butter, egg yolks and water. Mix until it forms a ball. By hand, mix flour and salt, cut in the butter, then combine water and egg yolks and add, mixing with a fork to form a soft ball. Chill at least 30 minutes before rolling, or wrap and freeze. This is a beautiful flaky pastry and so easy to handle.

Chef on the Run 33

Filling

> 3 tablespoons butter (45 mL)
> ½ onion, finely chopped
> ½ pound mushrooms (250 g)
> ¼ pound fresh shrimp (optional) (125 g)
> ¼ pound fresh crabmeat (optional) (125 g)
> 3 tablespoons finely chopped shallots or green onions (45 mL)
> 3 tablespoons white flour (45 mL)
> 1½ cups light cream (375 mL)
> pinches of nutmeg, salt and pepper
> 3 egg yolks
> 3 tablespoons chopped parsley (45 mL)

Melt butter in a heavy saucepan, add onion and cook over medium heat until soft but not brown. Stir in mushrooms and cook rapidly, stirring occasionally until all the moisture has evaporated. Do not overcook. Stir in the shallots or onions and continue cooking for about a minute longer. Stir in the flour, followed by cream, nutmeg, salt and pepper, and cook, stirring, until mixture thickens; then simmer for two minutes. Take saucepan from the heat and beat the egg yolks gradually into the hot mixture. Add parsley and crab and shrimp (if you are splurging). Taste for seasoning and let mixture cool in refrigerator.

Set oven to 400°F (200°C). Roll out two thirds of the dough to line a 9-inch (22 cm) pie pan or flan ring; prick the bottom lightly with a fork and chill. Spread cool filling in pie shell, roll out remaining dough and cut into thin strips. Lay a diagonal lattice over the filling, pressing the ends well down onto shell edge to seal. If necessary cover the edge with a strip of dough to make it neat. Brush lattice with egg glaze and bake for about 30 to 35 minutes until pastry is brown and filling starts to bubble. Cool then refrigerate, covered, overnight. Reheat in a 350°F (180°C) oven for about 30 minutes. The pie can also be frozen.

Salade Nicoise

This salad is a meal in itself. It is beautiful to look at and deliciously satisfying. The addition of cubed boiled potatoes, hard-cooked eggs, shrimp or any nice little leftovers will create a fine luncheon or light dinner entree. Serves 6 as side salad or 4 as entree.

2 small packets frozen green beans, French cut
    or 1½ pounds of fresh beans, sliced (750 g)
1 6½-ounce tin solid white tuna (184 g)
2 medium or 1 large cucumber
5 tomatoes, peeled
1 2-ounce tin anchovy fillets (50 g)
ripe olives

The day before serving, cook the beans for a minute or two, pour over a little French Dressing (see below) and marinate in the refrigerator overnight. On the day of serving, peel cucumbers, (unless they are English) cut three-quarters of them into chunks and the rest into paper-thin slices. Lay both on separate paper towels, sprinkle with salt and let stand for about 10 minutes. Pat dry. Cut three tomatoes into small chunks and the last two into small wedges. Soak anchovy in milk for about five minutes to remove salt flavour, then cut into very thin strips. Cut olives into cubes.

In an attractive glass bowl arrange beans, sliced tomatoes, cucumber chunks and tuna in layers, repeating about three times and moistening each layer with some of the French Dressing. Arrange slices of cucumber across the top, cover with a lattice of anchovy strips and decorate with black olives in the centre and tomato wedges around the outside.

French Dressing

1½ cups olive oil (375 mL)
1½ cups salad oil (375 mL)
⅓ cup white wine vinegar (75 mL)
1 clove garlic, pressed
½ teaspoon Dijon mustard (2 mL)
1 teaspoon sugar (5 mL)
juice of 1 lemon
½ teaspoon oregano (2 mL)
3 tablespoons chopped chives or green onions (30 mL)
3 teaspoons chopped shallots (optional) (15 mL)
2 tablespoons chopped parsley or dried chervil (30 mL)

Combine days ahead and store in the refrigerator. If you prefer a tarter dressing, add more lemon juice or vinegar.

Kahlua Mousse in Chocolate Cups

A coffee-flavoured cloud of a mousse with a crunchy toffee topping is served in small chocolate cups available from food specialty stores (or you can make your own). It can be made the day ahead and refrigerated. Serves 8.

2 eggs, separated
⅔ cup white sugar (150 mL)
1 cup strong warm coffee (250 mL)
2 small packages unflavoured gelatin
½ cup milk (125 mL)
½ cup Kahlua (125 mL)
1 pint whipping cream, whipped (500 mL)
2 tablespoons white sugar (30 mL)
10 Almond Roca bars, coarsely crushed

Beat egg yolks with ⅔ cup (150 mL) sugar, add coffee and stir well. Put in the top of a double boiler and cook until mixture coats a silver spoon — about 8 minutes. Set aside. Soak gelatin in milk in small saucepan and stir over very low heat until gelatin is dissolved. Add Kahlua and blend well. Add this mixture to the warm coffee custard and chill until partially set. It should be of the consistency of egg whites. Do not let it get too thick. Beat lightly with an electric mixer. Fold in whipped cream and whip until slightly fluffy. Beat egg whites until slightly stiff and slowly beat in 2 tablespoons (30 mL) sugar. Fold into coffee mixture. Put a little into each chocolate cup or into wine goblets. Refrigerate. Just before serving, sprinkle with crushed Almond Roca and offer additional Kahlua to pour over the top. If any mousse is left over after filling chocolate cups, put it in a bowl for second helpings.

Strawberries and Pineapple Grand Marnier

A marvellous addition to any buffet, this is at its best at the peak of the strawberry season.   Serves 6.

1 whole fresh pineapple
2 baskets fresh strawberries
Grand Marnier (or other orange liqueur)

In the afternoon of serving, slice the pineapple lengthwise, leaving the top leaves intact. Remove the core, scoop out the pineapple and slice into large cubes. Dry pineapple shells and set aside. Clean and dry the strawberries and take off the stems. In separate bowls marinate strawberries and pineapple cubes in enough Grand Marnier to cover and leave for at least three hours. To serve, pile marinated fruits into the pineapple shells and serve with toothpicks for guests to help themselves.

This dish is also great with fruit sherbert or Italian ice.

Super Soups

Crab Bisque
Clam or Seafood Chowder
Soupe au Pistou
Cold Avocado Soup
French Onion Soup
Gazpacho

There is nothing as satisfying, basic and down-to-earth as a hearty pot of home-made soup on a cold winter's day. Soups are a popular choice for informal brunches, dinners or even cocktail parties, with two or three different ones being offered along with assorted breads and cheeses and a platter of seasonal fruits. Hot soup in winter, cold soup in summer. My choice of a chilled soup is the nippy gazpacho and it keeps so well in the refrigerator that it is easy to have plenty on hand.

Crab Bisque

Quick to prepare, this is satin-smooth and creamy. Serve it in very small portions.
Serves 6.

8 ounces crab meat (250 g)
½ cup medium dry sherry (125 mL)
1 10-ounce can tomato soup (284 mL)
1 10-ounce can green pea soup (284 mL)
  (not the country style)
¼ teaspoon curry powder (1 mL)
¼ teaspoon paprika (1 mL)
squeeze of a lemon

On the morning of serving, marinate the crab in the sherry for about an hour in the refrigerator. Combine rest of ingredients in a saucepan and heat, but do not boil. Add to the crab meat and refrigerate. Before serving, reheat just to the boiling point. Top with a dollop of sour cream and a touch of dill weed.

Clam or Seafood Chowder

Chowder was originally a fisherman's stew of French origins, with salt pork or bacon being as essential an ingredient as the fish. New Englanders probably took their early recipe from French settlers in Canada, while the people of Manhattan Island varied theirs by adding tomatoes, and thus sparked the great chowder controversy which continues to this day. Whether you prefer Manhattan or New England style chowder, you'll like this one from the Canadian Maritimes. It adds white fish such as halibut or cod to the basic soup and should be served piping hot with tea biscuits instead of bread. (An extra cup of clams may be added instead of the fish.)   Serves 6.

> 4 slices bacon
>   or ¼ pound salt pork, cut into small cubes (125 g)
> 1 small onion, chopped
> 5 medium potatoes, peeled and cubed
> 3 tablespoons green pepper, chopped (optional) (45 mL)
> 2 stalks celery, chopped
> 2 carrots, chopped
> 1 clove garlic, crushed
> 2 cups chicken stock (500 mL)
> 1 teaspoon Worcestershire Sauce (5 mL)
> dash Tabasco (optional)
> salt and pepper to taste
> 3 cups raw baby clams with juice (750 mL)
>   or 2 14-ounce (398 mL) cans baby clams with juice
> 1 pint light cream (500 mL)
> 1½ pounds halibut or cod (750 g), cut into 1-inch (2.5 cm) cubes

In a large heavy saucepan saute the bacon or pork until crisp, add onion, potatoes, pepper, celery, carrots and garlic and saute for about two minutes. Add chicken stock, Worcestershire, Tabasco, salt and pepper. Cover saucepan and simmer for 15 minutes or until potatoes are tender. Mash the mixture slightly with potato masher.

   In a separate pan, heat clams in their juice for three minutes and add to the vegetables. Simmer the fish in one cup of water for about 4 minutes and add both fish and water to the soup pot. Stir in the light cream. Refrigerate until ready to serve, then reheat until hot.

Soupe au Pistou

This fresh vegetable soup is native to the French Riviera and is similar to the classic Italian minestrone. I make it frequently for weekend entertaining and just keep adding to the pot when hungry friends drop in without warning. A meal in itself, it is at its best made two days in advance. It is a thick soup but it can easily be thinned by adding chicken stock.

Serves 12

> ½ cup seashell macaroni (125 mL)
> 1 pound dry kidney or white beans (500 g)
> 5 quarts water (5 L)
> 4 slices meaty beef shanks, 1 inch (2.5 cm) thick
> 4 tablespoons salad oil (60 mL)
> 2 large onions, chopped
> 2 cups each diced carrots, celery, white part of leeks (500 mL)
> 1 28-ounce can solid pack tomatoes (796 mL)
> 3 medium potatoes, diced
> 2 cups fresh or frozen green beans (500 mL), cut into 2-inch (5 cm) pieces
> 3 small zucchini, unpeeled, cut lengthwise then sliced
> 3 cups shredded white cabbage (750 mL)
> Parmesan cheese, freshly grated
> Pistou (see below)

Cook macaroni in boiling water to cover until just tender. Drain, rinse with cold water and set aside. In a large Dutch oven, place the beans and water and bring to a boil. Boil for two minutes, remove from heat, cover and let stand for one hour. Add beef shanks, bring to boil again and simmer for 2 hours. Cool. Remove meat and bones. Remove half the beans and some of the stock and mash slightly. Return mashed beans to the pot. Discard beef bones and cut meat into cubes. Add to bean mixture and set aside.

Heat 4 tablespoons (60 mL) salad oil in a large frying pan. Add onions and saute until just tender. Then add carrots, celery and leeks, saute 5 minutes, then add canned tomatoes, chopped slightly, along with their juice. Simmer rapidly for about 10 minutes or until most of the liquid has evaporated. Add vegetable mixture to the beans and simmer for 30 minutes. Season to taste. Now add diced potatoes and green beans. Simmer rapidly, uncovered for 10 minutes, then add zucchini, cabbage and cooked macaroni. Simmer for 5 minutes more. Add pistou and blend well. Cover and refrigerate for one to two days for best flavour. Reheat through and serve sprinkled with fresh grated Parmesan cheese.

Pistou
Blend ½ cup (125 mL) chopped parsley in 2 tablespoons (30 mL) olive oil along with 3 tablespoons (45 mL) dried basil, a clove of garlic, minced, and 6 tablespoons (90 mL) tomato paste.

Cold Avocado Soup

This chilled soup is refreshing on a hot summer evening. Serve only about half a cup per serving as it is very rich. It can also be served hot.   Serves 8.

2 large ripe avocados
1 large firm avocado for garnish
4 cups chicken broth (1 L)
1 cup whipping cream (250 mL)
1 cup light cream (250 mL)
4 tablespoons white rum (60 mL)
½ teaspoon curry powder, or to taste (2 mL)
pinch salt and pepper
1 lemon, thinly sliced
1 lemon, in small wedges

A few hours before serving place two ripe avocados in blender or food processor along with all the rest of the ingredients except lemons and firm avocado. Blend until smooth, then cover and refrigerate. To serve, spoon into small bowls or sherbert dishes. Place a thin slice of avocado on top for garnish, then a thin slice of lemon. Pass lemon wedges.
    If serving hot, heat very gently until soup is hot but not boiling.

Onion Soup

The secret of a good onion soup is to cook the onions very slowly and to hold the soup for at least two days before serving to allow its flavours to mellow. I also prefer to use a combination of chicken and beef stock because I find that sometimes beef stock alone overpowers the onion flavour. The port or sherry gives this recipe a touch of class.

This soup often forms the basis for a complete meal, great for fireside entertaining. With it I serve crudites of vegetables with a herb dip (page 89) and a cheese fondue (page 88).   Serves 8 as a first course.

> 4 large white onions, sliced paper thin
> 3 tablespoons butter (45 mL)
> 2 tablespoons flour (30 mL)
> 4 cups beef stock (1 L)
>   or 3 10-ounce (284 mL) tins undiluted beef bouillon
> 2½ cups chicken stock (625 mL)
>   or 2 10-ounce (284 mL) tins undiluted chicken broth
> 2 cups water (500 mL)
> ⅓ cup port or medium dry sherry (75 mL)

For topping
> French bread
> Gruyere cheese, grated

In a heavy Dutch oven melt the butter and saute onions over very low heat for about 30 minutes or until golden. Add flour and blend, then add rest of ingredients. Simmer slowly for another 15 minutes. Store, covered, in the refrigerator for two days.

When ready to serve, heat soup to boiling and ladle into oven-proof soup bowls. Top each with a small piece of toasted French bread, sprinkle bread with a generous amount of freshly grated Gruyere cheese, place soup bowls on cookie sheet and heat in 325°F (160°C) oven for about 5 minutes or under the broiler until the cheese melts. Serve immediately.

If you find the onion flavour too strong, just add more water to the stock and if you want more flavour, use more onions. This soup freezes very well. Let it age for two days in the refrigerator then freeze it in three-cup (750 mL) containers.

Gazpacho

An old Spanish dish, this soup is a little like a salad with its crisp blend of vegetables and seasonings. Serve small portions as a first course or as the main course for a light lunch, along with French bread and cheese. My version is extra thick, with lots of chunky textures.   Serves 8 to 10.

4 very ripe large tomatoes
1 14-ounce can tomatoes, drained (398 mL)
½ small onion
1 English cucumber, unpeeled
   or 1 regular cucumber, peeled
½ large green pepper, seeded
4 sprigs parsley
1 clove garlic, crushed
10 ounces V-8 juice (284 mL)
1½ to 2 cups tomato juice (375 to 500 mL)
½ tablespoon lemon juice (7 mL)
3 tablespoons salad oil (45 mL)
¼ to ½ cup chili sauce (50 to 125 mL)
¼ teaspoon basil (1 mL)
⅛ teaspoon oregano (0.5 mL)
½ teaspoon Hungarian sweet paprika (2 mL)
1 tablespoon white wine vinegar (15 mL)
¼ to ½ teaspoon Worcestershire Sauce (1 to 2 mL)

At least 3 days before serving, cut tomatoes, onion, cucumber and green pepper into chunks and put them through a food processor or chop in blender with parsley, garlic, V-8 juice and tomato juice, processing a portion at a time. Add rest of ingredients and blend. Do not over-process for you want to keep the mixture chunky. Cover and refrigerate. This soup improves with age and will keep for at least five days.

   Serve in small bowls or sherbert dishes along with croutons, chopped tomatoes or chopped chives. If you prefer a thinner soup, add more tomato juice and experiment with herbs and seasonings until the soup is to your liking.

Mediterranean Medley

Sangria de Granada
Bagna Cauda
Assorted Vegetables
Breadsticks
Paella or Bouillabaisse
Orange and Avocado Salad
Coffee Cream Torte
Red or White Bordeaux wine

The foods of the Mediterranean are tangy, bold and colourful. The shores of Spain and Portugal specialize in seafood dishes, two of the most outstanding contributions being Paella and Bouillabaisse. I have adapted both recipes for seafood available in Canada from coast to coast.

This dinner, which begins with Spanish sangria, is casual in tempo with guests helping themselves. The light liqueur-soaked cake is an excellent choice for dessert and always rates second helpings.

Sangria de Granada

It is best to make the sangria early in the day or at least three to four hours ahead of serving so the flavours will mingle. It's very popular on a hot evening.
12 servings

1 orange
¼ cup white sugar (50 mL)
2 cups fresh orange juice (500 mL)
1 26-ounce bottle dry red wine (750 mL)
½ cup Cointreau, Grand Marnier
    or other orange-flavoured liqueur (125 mL)
sliced oranges, peeled
sliced apples
sliced lemons

With a vegetable peeler, thinly cut off the outer peel or zest of half the orange. In a bowl, rub the sugar over the peel with your hands to release the flavourful oils. Add orange juice, red wine and orange liqueur, cover and chill. Remove the orange peel after the first 15 minutes, then add the fruit.

Serve in a punch bowl or pitcher, adding a few pieces of fruit, some ice cubes and a squirt of soda to each drink.

Bagna Cauda

A typical Spanish appetizer, the bagna cauda reposes among vegetables and breadsticks for dipping. Watch it disappear. Even those who claim not to like anchovies will enjoy the dip's subtle flavour.   Serves 6 to 8.

1 pint whipping cream (500 mL)
4 tablespoons butter (60 mL)
8 flat anchovy fillets
1 garlic clove, crushed

In a three or four-cup (.75 to 1 L) enamelled casserole or saucepan bring the cream to a boil and simmer, stirring frequently, for about 40 minutes or until thickened. There should be about 1 cup (250 mL) remaining. This stage can be done just before the guests arrive; set the pot aside but do not refrigerate or it will turn to butter when you reheat. Drain anchovy fillets, rinse them in milk to eliminate some of the salt and chop finely. Melt butter in a chafing dish that fits over a candle but do not allow to become brown. Add anchovies, garlic and thickened cream, blend well until just warmed and serve at once. Keep warm over a candle.

Serve with bread sticks and an assortment of vegetables, prepared ahead of time and displayed on a bed of romaine lettuce. Some suggestions: cucumbers, carrots, red and green peppers and celery, all cut into thin, 2-inch (5 cm) strips; green onions, cauliflower buds, cherry tomatoes, zucchini, broccoli flowerets etc.

Bouillabaisse

The American version of Bouillabaisse is known as Cioppino and legend explains the name this way: As Portuguese fishermen steered their boats into San Francisco harbour, a cry of "chip in" went up and each boat made its contribution to the pot of fish stew bubbling on the wharf. This hearty stew is best with fresh fish right off the docks but frozen fish may be substituted. You can start the dish the day before and add the seafood 30 minutes before serving.   Serves 6 to 8.

½ cup salad oil or olive oil (125 mL)
2 cloves garlic, crushed
2 onions, chopped
1 green pepper, diced
2 28-ounce (796 mL) cans tomatoes
1 14-ounce can tomato sauce (398 mL)
3 cups dry white wine (750 mL)
⅓ cup parsley, chopped (75 mL)
½ teaspoon oregano (2 mL)
½ teaspoon basil (2 mL)
dash pepper
1½ cups water or tomato juice (375 mL)
lemon wedges
parsley
1½ pounds halibut or red snapper
     or combination (750 g)
16 clams or 1 10-ounce can whole baby clams (284 mL)
     or 16 mussels in shells
½ pound scallops (250 g)
1 pound medium shrimp, shelled (500 g)
½ pound crab legs or lobster meat for garnish, optional (250 g)

The night before serving, heat oil in a 6-quart kettle and saute the garlic, onions and pepper until limp. Add undrained tomatoes, tomato sauce, wine, parsley, oregano, pepper, basil, water or tomato juice. Bring to a boil then simmer, uncovered, for about 25 minutes, stirring occasional-ly. Cover and refrigerate. Prepare the fish the following morning. Cut halibut or snapper into 1½-inch (4 cm) pieces and refrigerate until 30 minutes before serving. Reheat stock, add clams or mussels and bring to a boil; simmer until shellfish opens. Add halibut or red snapper chunks, scallops and shrimp and simmer, covered, about 10 minutes. Uncover and simmer for an additional 10 minutes. Add crab legs or lobster just before serving. Sprinkle with parsley, correct seasoning and serve with lemon wedges.

Paella

The traditional Spanish paella derives its name from the shallow open pan in which it is cooked, though a large heavy skillet can be used instead. Each region of Spain has its own version but all add saffron which gives this dish a brilliant yellow colour and a unique flavour. Best with fresh seafood, frozen seafood can also be used, but canned goods do not do this dish justice. I cook my version of Paella in the oven rather than on the stove as it is done in Spain.   Serves 8 to 10.

¼ cup olive oil (50 mL)
2 chicken breasts, boned, skinned and cut into 1-inch (2.5 cm) pieces
½ pound chorizo or cocktail sausage, cut into pieces (250 g)
1 pound boneless pork (500 g), cut into 1-inch (2.5 cm) pieces
1 large onion, finely chopped
1 green pepper, cut into thin strips
¼ pound mushrooms, sliced (125 g)
2 cloves garlic, crushed
¼ teaspoon saffron powder (1 mL)
pinches oregano, salt and pepper
3 cups long-grained rice (750 mL)
8 cups chicken stock (2 L)
¼ cup brandy (50 mL)
½ pound red snapper or other white fish (250 g), cut into 2-inch (5 cm)
    pieces and/or ½ pound scallops (250 g)
1 pound raw prawns, peeled (500 g)
1½ cups frozen peas (375 mL)
2 medium tomatoes, peeled and cubed

Early in the morning or the night before, heat olive oil in pan and saute the chicken, sausage and pork until golden. Set aside. Then saute onions, green peppers and mushrooms, adding more oil if necessary.

Add garlic, saffron, oregano and rice and stir for about 5 minutes. Blend with the meats and refrigerate.

Half an hour before guests arrive, heat oven to 400°F (200°C). Add stock, brandy and fish or scallops to the meat and rice mixture in your large pan; salt and pepper to taste. Bring to a boil, cover with foil and put into oven. Bake about 20 to 25 minutes, then add prawns. Stir slightly, about every five minutes. Add peas and tomatoes and bake another 5 to 10 minutes or until prawns are cooked and the stock is just about all absorbed. Do not overcook; the paella must be moist. Add more chicken stock if necessary. To serve, decorate top with wedges of lemon, strips of pimento, ripe olives and parsley and let everyone dig in.

Orange and Avocado Salad

Bring in this refreshing salad either before or after the main course.

Serves 8 well.

1 medium size sweet onion
assorted greens, 4 heads
3 large oranges, peeled
2 large avocados, peeled and cubed
½ cup sunflower seeds, toasted (125 mL)
½ cup pecans or walnuts, toasted (125 mL)

Peel and slice the onion into thin rings. Slice the oranges and combine with the onions. Pour over some of the dressing and refrigerate for a few hours. Just before serving, break up salad greens into bowl, add prepared oranges and onions, plus avocado cubes, sunflower seeds and nuts. Add more dressing, toss well and serve.

To toast nuts: spread on a cookie tray and heat in a 350°F (180°C) oven for about 5 to 8 minutes until golden. Watch carefully lest they burn. Store in plastic bags until needed.

Dressing

⅓ cup salad oil (75 mL)
  or half salad oil and half olive oil
1 teaspoon sugar (5 mL)
1 tablespoon wine vinegar (15 mL)
2 teaspoons grated orange peel (10 mL)
¼ cup undiluted frozen orange juice (50 mL)
¼ cup orange liqueur (50 mL)

Mix all together and store in refrigerator. This may be made the day before.

Coffee Cream Torte

This superb cake was first introduced to me by my sister-in-law Dianne. It has become a special treat for birthdays, anniversaries and other special occasions. It should be prepared the day before to let the flavours mingle — which is perfect for the busy hostess.   Serves 12 to 16.

Cake

4 large eggs
1 cup whole milk (250 mL)
3 tablespoons butter (45 mL)
pinch salt
2 cups white sugar (500 mL)
2 cups all purpose flour (500 mL)
2 teaspoons baking powder (10 mL)
2 teaspoons vanilla (10 mL)

In medium size bowl, beat eggs until pale yellow and thick, about 5 minutes. Add salt, vanilla and sugar gradually, beating until fluffy. Heat milk until warm, and add butter, stirring until butter melts. Add to eggs and beat for one minute. Blend flour and baking powder and gently fold into the batter. Line two 8-inch (20 cm) round cake pans with wax paper. Divide cake mixture between both and bake at 350°F (180°C) for about 25 minutes or until done. They will be thin. Remove cakes from pan, cool, wrap and store in refrigerator. (Cakes can be frozen for future use.)

Sauce

1 cup double-strength coffee (250 mL)
   (5 teaspoons (25 mL) instant coffee plus 1 cup (250 mL) water)
1 cup white sugar (250 mL)
6 tablespoons white rum (90 mL)

Filling

1 pint whipping cream (500 mL)
2 tablespoons white rum or Tia Maria (30 mL)
2 tablespoons white sugar (30 mL)

¾ cup Tia Maria (200 mL)

Make sauce by mixing coffee with sugar until blended and heating slowly until it comes to a boil. Simmer for about 15 minutes. Add white rum. Set aside to cool.

Whip cream with 2 tablespoons (30 mL) liquor and sugar and set aside until ready to assemble cake.

Cut each cake into two layers. Place one layer, cut side up, on serving plate and drizzle over about 4 tablespoons (60 mL) of the coffee syrup and 4 tablespoons (60 mL) of Tia Maria. Spread over about 1 cup (250 mL) of whipped cream. Repeat this process with the other two layers. Glaze top layer with remaining coffee syrup and spread remaining cream on sides of cake. Refrigerate overnight. This cake can be served with ice cream, either vanilla or coffee. Slice in very thin wedges. Any leftovers will freeze beautifully.

Hawaiian Christmas Luau

Pali Punch
Six Assorted Hawaiian Pupus (Hors d'oeuvres)
Chicken Hawaiian
Beef Tenderloin Teriyaki
Shrimp-stuffed Red Snapper
Polynesian Rice Mingle
Fruit Kebabs
Island Salad Bar
Mai Tai Souffle
Hawaiian Sundaes with Chocolate Fondue Sauce
California Chablis and California Burgundy

Although winter cold never reaches Hawaii, Christmas on the islands follows the traditions set by New England missionaries who arrived there 160 years ago. Churches re-enact the nativity scene and traditional carols are sung in English — and holiday foods are steamed, fried and baked by island cooks. Hawaiian cooking is always an adventure for it includes food from all the many different ethnic groups that settled there. This exotic and lavish menu is truly a feast, resplendent with tropical fruit and fresh orchids. It can be simplified by reducing the number of dishes. Previously featured in *Western Living magazine*, this complete presentation was duplicated by a group of magazine readers on holiday in Hawaii. Each family made two or three of the items and brought them to the feast. They said it was a smash hit!

Pali Punch

A colorful and refreshing punch, this would be a good opener for any party.

Serves 18 to 20

9 cups fresh orange juice (2.25 L)
¾ cup white creme de cacao (200 mL)
¼ cup fresh lemon juice (50 mL)
3 cups white rum (750 mL)
½ cup Cointreau or other orange-flavoured liqueur (125 mL)
2 cups pineapple juice (500 mL)
2 tablespoons grenadine syrup (optional) (30 mL)

Blend well a few hours before serving and chill. Pour over crushed ice in tall glasses and decorate with sprigs of fresh mint and slices of orange, pineapple, lime or lemon. It may also be served in a punch bowl.

Hawaiian Pupus

A lavish feast such as this should begin slowly and leisurely, giving guests time to mingle. Serve several pupus or appetizers from this array of hot and cold varieties, all of them delicious.

Rumaki

Makes 32.

16 slices bacon
3 tablespoons soy sauce (45 mL)
2 teaspoons sugar (10 mL)
Pinch of ginger
1 pound chicken livers, cut into small pieces (500 g)
1 cup water chestnuts, cut in half (250 mL)

Cut bacon strips in half and fry till partially cooked and still soft. Combine soy sauce, sugar and ginger and pour over the chicken livers. Leave to marinate for 20 minutes. Wrap pieces of liver and water chestnuts in bacon strips, skewering in place with toothpicks. Place on rack in 450°F (230°C) oven for about 10 minutes or broil until brown.

Lomi Lomi Salmon Tomatoes

Makes 2 to 3 dozen.

1 box cherry tomatoes
¼ pound smoked salmon or lox, finely chopped (125 g)
2 green onions, finely chopped
1 green pepper, finely chopped
dash pepper
squeeze of lemon juice
2 tablespoons chopped parsley (30 mL)

Cut off and discard the tops of tomatoes and cut a very thin slice off the bottoms so they will sit steadily. Remove pulp from insides and pat insides dry. Cover and refrigerate. Combine tomato pulp, well chopped, with the rest of ingredients, cover and chill. Fill tomatoes with the stuffing about two or three hours before serving and arrange on lettuce leaves on serving platter.

Oriental Meatballs

Serves 8.

1 14-ounce can pineapple tidbits (398 mL)
1 pound ground beef (500 g)
2 tablespoons chopped onion (30 mL)
½ cup fine bread crumbs (125 mL)
1 tablespoon chopped parsley (15 mL)
pinches of salt, pepper, curry powder
1 egg
⅔ cup milk (150 mL)
butter and oil for frying
Sweet-Sour Sauce

Take out 32 tidbits, reserve rest along with syrup. Combine beef with rest of ingredients and let stand, covered, in refrigerator for one hour. Roll into balls around pieces of pineapple, heat butter and oil (enough to coat the pan) and brown meatballs well. Drain off fat, add Sweet-Sour Sauce and cook until thick. Add remaining tidbits (save the syrup) and heat another 5 minutes. This can be made the day ahead and reheated at 350°F (180°C) for about 25 to 30 minutes. Serve with cocktail picks.

Sweet-Sour Sauce

Blend ½ cup (125 mL) of reserved pineapple syrup with ⅛ cup (25 mL) white wine vinegar, ¼ cup (50 mL) brown sugar, 1 tablespoon (15 mL) cornstarch, a pinch of salt and 1 teaspoon (5 mL) soy sauce. Cook until thickened, stirring constantly.

King Crab Fruit Tray

This unique salad makes an outstanding luncheon dish for a hot summer day. Serves 4 to 6.

1 pound Alaska king crab meat, cooked (500 g)
* or crab legs, or mixture of crab and prawns*
2 small pineapples
3 avocados
juice of 1 lemon
1 cantaloupe, peeled, in wedges
1 honeydew melon, peeled, in wedges
2 to 3 10-ounce (284 g) cans mandarin oranges, drained
salad greens
green grapes

An hour or two before serving, peel pineapples, remove eyes and slice into ½-inch (12 mm) thick rounds. Discard core and cut rest into small cubes. Line a large platter with lettuce and arrange the fruit and crabmeat in rows. Leave the avocado until just before serving. Peel and cut in slices, then dip in lemon juice to prevent darkening. Decorate platter with clusters of grapes. Seal well and refrigerate until just before serving with bowls of sauce for dipping and chopped macadamia nuts for garnish.

Sauce

½ pint sour cream (250 mL)
juice and rind of 1 small lime
¼ cup fruit chutney, chopped fine (50 mL)
macadamia nuts, chopped

Combine everything but the nuts and refrigerate in sealed container. When ready to serve, place in attractive dish and sprinkle with nuts.

Pineapple-Shrimp Boats

Serves 8.

1 whole pineapple
¾ to 1 pound large shrimp or prawn,
    cooked and shelled (400-500 g)

Cut pineapple lengthwise across the top ¼-inch (6 mm) down, leaving green leaves intact. Scoop out pineapple, remove core and cut into cubes. Spear cubes of pineapple and pieces of shrimp with skewers and place around the pineapple rim. Pour heated Polynesian Sauce into the pineapple shell and let guests help themselves.

Polynesian Sauce

1 12-ounce jar apricot preserves (375 mL)
2 tablespoons cider or wine vinegar (30 mL)
1 8-ounce tin crushed pineapple (250 mL)
1 teaspoon Worcestershire Sauce (5 mL)
½ cup tomato ketchup (125 mL)
pinch ginger
pinch mustard

Combine all ingredients, heat to boiling and pour into pineapple shell.

Macadamia Nut Cheese Biscuits

Makes about 3 dozen.

½ pound butter, softened (250 g)
¼ pound Swiss cheese, grated (125 g)
1 egg
½ teaspoon salt (2 mL)
1½ cups white flour (375 mL)
⅓ cup chopped macadamia nuts (75 mL)

Blend butter, cheese and egg and gradually work in flour, salt and nuts. Mold into a roll 1½ inches (4 cm) in diameter; wrap in wax paper and chill until firm. Slice dough into ¼-inch (6 mm) rounds and bake on lightly buttered cookie sheets in 400°F (200°C) oven for about 10 to 15 minutes or until lightly browned. If you make this ahead, reheat at 400°F (200°C) for a few minutes just before serving.

Chicken Hawaiian

This can be prepared weeks ahead of time and frozen. It serves 12 at buffet or 8 as entree.

> 8 chicken breasts (double)
> ¼ cup soy sauce (50 mL)
> ½ cup dry white wine (125 mL)
> juice of 1 lime
> 1 clove garlic, crushed
> ⅛ teaspoon ginger (0.5 mL)
>   or ½ teaspoon minced ginger root (2 mL)
> pinch of thyme
> pinch of oregano
> dash of pepper (no salt)
> ½ teaspoon curry powder (2 mL)

Remove bones and skin from chicken and cut each single breast into two, making 32 pieces. Mix together rest of ingredients, pour over chicken in a large bowl and marinate for 2 to 3 hours, turning occasionally. Remove chicken, dust lightly with flour (save marinade) and brown both sides in butter in large frypan. Do not overcook. Use more butter as needed to brown all the pieces. Place chicken in a single layer in large casserole dish.

In the same frypan, melt about 3 tablespoons (45 mL) butter and sauté 2 medium onions, thinly sliced, until light yellow. Sprinkle onion rings over chicken, then pour over the reserved marinade. At this stage the chicken can be sealed well and frozen; otherwise cover and refrigerate overnight. Bake, covered, at 350°F (180°C) for 30 minutes, then uncover, pour over ¼ cup (50 mL) dry white wine and bake for another 10 to 15 minutes until cooked. Serve around bed of Polynesian Rice Mingle, alternated with Fruit Kebabs.

Polynesian Rice Mingle

Wild rice is blended with white rice, seasoned with chicken stock and soy sauce, then topped with macadamia nuts for a dish that goes well with all the entrees, the chicken, steak and fish. It also makes a great stuffing for poultry and roasts.   Serves 8 to 10.

¾ cup wild rice (200 mL)
1¼ cups Uncle Ben's long-grain rice (325 mL)
⅔ cup butter (150 mL)
4 cups chicken stock (1 L)
dash garlic salt
3 tablespoons minced green onions (45 mL)
3 tablespoons soy sauce (45 mL)
½ cup coarsely chopped macadamia nuts (125 mL)
chopped parsley

Put wild and white rice in a casserole dish and pour over enough boiling water to cover. Let sit about 30 minutes, then strain rice and rinse well with cold water until all starch is removed. Drain well. Melt the butter in a large casserole, add drained rice and stir over medium heat until all the butter is absorbed — about 5 minutes. Pour chicken stock over the rice and sprinkle with garlic salt, green onion and soy sauce. Stir well. Cover and refrigerate for up to two days ahead of time, or overnight.

On the day of serving, remove casserole from the refrigerator two hours before baking. Stir rice gently and bake at 375°F (190°C) for about 1½ hours. Seal casserole well with aluminum foil under the lid to keep it airtight. Check rice after an hour — it must not dry out. When done, the rice should have absorbed all the liquid and be light and fluffy. Sprinkle with macadamia nuts and parsley and garnish with slices of orange.

Fruit Kebabs

A colorful and tropical accompaniment to the chicken and rice.

> 4 to 5 sweet potatoes
> ½ cup butter (125 mL)
> 1 cup brown sugar (250 mL)
> 1 14-ounce can pineapple chunks (398 mL)
> 1 large banana
> lemon juice
> pieces of lime

Bake sweet potatoes in 350°F (180°C) oven until tender. Melt butter and put into bowl. Place brown sugar in another bowl. Peel sweet potatoes and cut into large cubes. Drain pineapple; peel and slice banana and dip in lemon juice. Dip everything in butter, then in brown sugar. Spear pieces of potato and fruit on skewers, one for each guest, and top each with a piece of lime. Place skewers in casserole dish and heat at 350°F (180°C) for 10 to 15 minutes. Arrange on platter with chicken and rice.

Shrimp-Stuffed Red Snapper

A whole baked fish is always the star attraction at a buffet and this one tastes as good as it looks.   Serves 8 to 12.

> ⅓ cup butter (75 mL)
> ⅓ cup oil (75 mL)
> 3 tablespoons butter (45 mL)
> 1½ cups soft fresh breadcrumbs (375 mL)
> 3 tablespoons dry white wine (45 mL)
> 3 tablespoons chopped parsley (45 mL)
> pinches of onion salt and nutmeg
> ½ pound cooked baby shrimp (250 g)
> 1 large egg yolk
> ¼ cup soft butter (50 mL)
> 1 4-to-5 pound whole red snapper, cleaned,
>   with head and tail intact (2 to 2.5 kg)

Melt butter with oil and use half to grease a large baking dish. Set remainder aside. Melt the 3 tablespoons (45 mL) butter in a medium skillet, add breadcrumbs and saute briefly until golden brown. Transfer to a medium bowl, add wine, parsley, onion salt, nutmeg and shrimp. Mix with wooden spoon until stuffing mixture is well blended and beat in the egg yolk.

Preheat oven to 375°F (190°C). Stuff fish cavity and close opening with small metal skewers. Place fish in prepared baking pan and brush with reserved butter-oil mixture. Bake uncovered for about 35 minutes or until flesh flakes easily. Carefully transfer to a large platter and garnish with parsley, lemon and lime slices and ripe olives.

Beef Tenderloin Teriyaki

Though at its best made just prior to serving, this Chinese-style dish made in a wok can also be prepared ahead of time and reheated.

Serves 8.

2 pounds boned beef tenderloin (1 kg)
3 tablespoons olive oil (45 mL)
6 tablespoons butter (90 mL)
salt and pepper
dashes of sage and cumin
1½ pounds mushrooms, quartered (750 g)
2 cloves garlic, crushed
2 medium size onions, in wedges
2 medium size green peppers, seeded, in 2 inch pieces
4 to 5 medium tomatoes, peeled and seeded, in wedges
¼ cup soy sauce (50 mL)
1 tablespoon cider vinegar (15 mL)
2 tablespoons tomato paste (30 mL)
¼ cup medium sherry or red wine (50 mL)
2 tablespoons brown sugar (30 mL)

Slice beef into paper thin strips, each about 3 inches (8 cm) by 2 inches (5 cm). Saute quickly a few strips at a time in 1½ tablespoons (25 mL) olive oil and 3 tablespoons (45 mL) butter in a large wok or fry pan. Sprinkle with salt, pepper, sage and cumin and set aside. Saute the mushrooms, then the garlic, onions, green peppers and tomatoes in the remaining butter and oil and add to the meat. In the same pan, combine soy sauce, vinegar and tomato sauce, add wine and brown sugar and bring to boil. Pour over the meat and vegetables and saute gently to mix. Serve immediately with the rice. If you prepare this dish ahead, reheat at 350°F (180°C) for 25 minutes or until hot.

Island Salad Bar Gourmet Eight

This is one of the recipes from the cookbook our local Gourmet 8 club published a few years ago. It's a great serve-it-yourself salad with a tropical air, accompanied by two kinds of dressing.   Serves 8.

> 1 19-ounce can grapefruit sections, drained (540 mL)
> 4 kiwi fruit, peeled and sliced
> 1 or 2 10-ounce cans mandarin oranges, drained (284 mL)
> 1 14-ounce can artichoke hearts, sliced (398 mL)
>   or 1 14-ounce can hearts of palm, sliced
> 1 cup chopped green onion (250 mL)
> 1 cup shredded medium Cheddar cheese (250 mL)
> 1 cup chopped celery (250 mL)
> 1 cup chopped macadamia nuts (250 mL)

Select all or a few of the ingredients and place in small bowls. Fill a large salad bowl full of assorted greens such as romaine and butter lettuce and endive, and present everything on a large tray,along with the two types of dressing.

Avocado Dressing
> 1 ripe avocado
> 1 tablespoon lemon juice (15 mL)
> 1/2 cup sour cream (125 mL)
> 7 tablespoons salad oil (105 mL)
> pinch garlic salt
> 1/4 teaspoon Worcestershire Sauce (1 mL)
> 1/2 teaspoon sugar (2 mL)
> salt and pepper

Mash avocado in blender, add rest of ingredients and mix well. Make about an hour before serving.

Hawaiian French Dressing

¼ cup white wine vinegar (50 mL)
½ teaspoon salt (2 mL)
pinch dry mustard
1 teaspoon white sugar (5 mL)
dash of pepper
¾ cup salad oil (200 mL)
¼ cup pineapple juice (50 mL)
½ to 1 teaspoon crushed dry mint (2 to 5 mL)
or ¼ cup minced fresh mint (50 mL)

Blend vinegar with dry ingredients, then mix in oil, pineapple juice and mint. Shake well and chill before using. This can be made the day ahead of serving but will need to be well shaken.

Mai Tai Souffle

A light and refreshing finale to any meal, this looks regally Hawaiian decorated with fresh baby orchids.   Serves 10 to 12.

10 eggs, separated
2 cups white sugar (500 mL)
½ cup fresh lime juice (125 mL)
¼ cup fresh lemon juice (50 mL)
¼ cup Curacao or other orange liqueur (50 mL)
pinch salt
2 envelopes unflavoured gelatin
¼ cup light rum (50 mL)
¼ cup medium or dark rum (50 mL)
3 cups whipping cream (750 mL)
1 tablespoon light or dark rum (15 mL)
1 tablespoon icing sugar (15 mL)

Beat egg yolks until lemon coloured and fluffy. Gradually add 1 cup (250 ml) of sugar and beat until smooth. Add lime and lemon juices and a pinch of salt and beat until thoroughly blended. Soak gelatin in rum and dissolve over low heat. Place beaten yolks in saucepan over low heat and stir until slightly thickened. Gradually mix in the rum-gelatin mixture, then cool.

Oil a six-cup (1.5 L) souffle dish and wrap top with an oiled strip of wax paper or foil to form a collar. Beat egg whites until slightly stiff, then gradually add remaining cup of sugar and beat until very stiff. Whip 2 cups (500 mL) cream until thick and fold into cooled custard, then fold in the beaten egg whites. Put mixture into souffle dish and chill overnight. A few hours before serving, whip remaining cup (250 mL) of cream, adding to it the rum and icing sugar. Remove collar from souffle and decorate top with cream, mint leaves, baby orchids or lemon curls.

Hawaiian Sundaes with Chocolate Fondue Sauce

Impressive and fun to make, this is a self-serve sundae bar with a delicious fondue sauce.

> 1 fresh pineapple
> ½ cup fine white sugar (125 mL)
> ½ cup dark rum (125 mL)
> ½ cup toasted coconut (125 mL)
> ½ cup chopped macadamia nuts (125 mL)
> 1 fresh pineapple, cored and cubed
>   or 1 large can pineapple chunks
> 5 oranges, peeled and sectioned
>   or 2 tins mandarin oranges
> chocolate fondue sauce
> coconut syrup
> vanilla and macadamia nut ice cream

Fill large glass or clear plastic bowl with crushed ice. Cut top off pineapple and hollow out enough of the flesh to accommodate a can of canned heat. Place pineapple in crushed ice and surround with separate bowls of sugar, rum, toasted coconut and nuts. Place mounds of pineapple chunks and orange sections on tray along with bowls of chocolate fondue sauce, coconut syrup, balls of vanilla and macadamia nut ice cream and a supply of skewers. Set canned heat alight. Each guests skewers some fruit, dips it in rum, then sugar and caramelizes it over the flame. The fruit is eaten with ice cream and choice of toppings and can also be dipped in the chocolate or coconut sauces.

Mediterranean Medley, page 44.
Overleaf, Hawaiian Christmas Luau, page

Chocolate Fondue Sauce

1 6-ounce package chocolate chips (150 g)
¼ cup light cream (50 mL)
½ teaspoon vanilla extract (2 mL)
3 tablespoons Tia Maria (45 mL)

In heavy saucepan over gentle heat melt the chocolate chips, stirring often. Stir in cream, vanilla and liqueur. This can also be served as the sauce for a traditional fruit fondue with bananas, strawberries, oranges and pineapple. It can be made ahead and stored in the refrigerator, then reheated just before serving.

Picnic in the Park

Gazpacho (page 43)
Brie Cheese and Fresh Fruit
Ham Cornucopias stuffed with Chicken Parmesan Fingers
Marinated Zucchini Salad
Tabbouleh Salad
French Bread and Croissants
Chocolate Brownie Cookies
Blueberry Tart
Sparkling wine and mineral water, on ice

Champagne was popping everywhere as picnic baskets were opened in London's Hyde Park. The occasion was the fireworks display on the eve of the wedding of Prince Charles and Lady Diana — and the crowd was in a festive mood. We had selected several picnic foods from Harrod's famous food floor and relaxed along with 500,000 other spectators to watch the show.

Few picnics could match such a historic occasion or setting but they are fun anywhere. Vancouver's Stanley Park is one of my favourite places. This carefree picnic menu travels well and will satisfy those ravenous outdoor appetites.

Top, Seafood & Mushroom Pie and Salad Nicoise,
from A Morning Affair, page 30.
Bottom, Fitness Feast, page 95.

Ham Cornucopias with Chicken Parmesan Fingers

These are not only attractive, they are delicious! Chicken fingers are breaded with Parmesan cheese and seasonings, then wrapped in baked ham coated with a herbed cheese sauce. The chicken fingers could also be served alone. Allow two or three per person.   Serves 8.

> 14 slices of baked ham, ¼-inch thick (6 mm)
> 1 cup cream cheese, softened (250 mL)
> ½ teaspoon dill weed (2 mL)
> juice of ½ lemon
> ½ teaspoon Dijon mustard (2 mL)
> 4 single chicken breasts, skinned and deboned
> 1½ cups fine dry bread crumbs (375 mL)
> ⅔ cup Parmesan cheese, approx. (150 mL)
> lemon pepper
> melted butter

Cut each slice of ham into 4-inch (10 cm) squares. Combine cream cheese with seasonings and spread about 1 tablespoon (15 mL) over one side of each square of ham. Cut each chicken breast into 5-6 fingers, each ½ inch (12 mm) by 4 inches (10 cm). Dip into beaten eggs then roll in bread crumbs mixed with cheese and lemon pepper. Saute in enough butter to coat the pan until chicken is cooked and crispy. This should take only about 3 minutes on each side. Do not overcook. Drain on paper towels. Place a strip of the cooled chicken on one of the corners of the ham squares, then fold in the three other corners to form a cornucopia. Secure with cocktail picks if necessary. Decorate top with a little parsley, cover and refrigerate. To serve, arrange on bed of lettuce on a platter and garnish with stuffed eggs, black and green olives and carrot sticks.

Marinated Zucchini Salad

This is grand for picnics as it marinates overnight without going limp. Toss gently with a little extra dressing just before serving. Placed in a hollowed-out large cabbage, it makes a stunning centrepiece.

4 to 5 medium sized zucchini, sliced 1/4-inch (6 mm) thick
1/2 pound medium sized mushrooms, sliced (250 g)
1/2 cup ripe olives, pitted (125 mL)
1/2 cup natural sunflower seeds, toasted (125 mL)

Sprinkle zucchini slices with a little salt and let stand 5 minutes. Pat dry with paper towels. Place zucchini and mushrooms in separate bowls and pour over just enough of the dressing to coat well. Cover and refrigerate overnight. Turn into salad bowl, add olives and sunflower seeds and toss with additional dressing.

Dressing

2 cups salad oil (500 mL)
8 tablespoons tarragon or white wine vinegar (120 mL)
2 teaspoons Dijon mustard (10 mL)
2 teaspoons basil (10 mL)
2 tablespoons finely chopped parsley (30 mL)
4 tablespoons finely chopped green onion (60 mL)
2 tablespoons chervil (30 mL)
salt and pepper

Combine all ingredients; shake well to blend.

Tabbouleh Salad

This is a bulgar (cracked wheat) and tomato salad from Middle Eastern cuisine. The bulgar adds a pleasant crunchiness to the salad which for picnics can be served rolled up in lettuce leaves for easy munching.

Serves 8.

1 cup fine bulgar or cracked wheat (250 mL)
¼ cup chopped fresh mint (50 mL)
    or 1 tablespoon dried mint leaves (15 mL)
4 large tomatoes, peeled, finely chopped
½ cup peeled chopped cucumber (125 mL)
1 cup finely chopped parsley (250 mL)
4 green onions, finely chopped
½ green pepper, finely chopped
    and/or red pepper, finely chopped
¼ cup toasted sesame seeds (50 mL)
½ cup chopped walnuts (125 mL)

Soak bulgar in enough boiling water to cover for about 30 to 40 minutes. Rinse in a strainer, drain well and squeeze dry in cheesecloth or clean dish towel. Place in large salad bowl. Combine with rest of ingredients, add dressing and toss well. Adjust seasoning, adding more lemon juice if desired. Cover and refrigerate 2 or 3 days before serving — it improves with sitting. Garnish with additional tomato wedges and fresh mint.

Dressing
1 clove garlic, crushed
½ cup olive oil (125 mL)
½ cup lemon juice (125 mL)
salt and pepper
¼ teaspoon cinnamon (1 mL)

Combine all ingredients and beat well to mix.

Chocolate Brownie Cookies

This is a cake-like brownie baked as cookies. The sour cream lends a moist texture. This recipe has been in my files for more than 20 years and it never fails to please. The cookies are great for packing in lunches and they freeze well. Makes about 2½ dozen.

½ cup butter (125 mL)
1 cup brown sugar (250 mL)
1 egg
1 teaspoon vanillla (5 mL)
2 1-ounce squares unsweetened chocolate, melted (50 g)
2 cups flour (500 mL)
½ teaspoon baking soda (2 mL)
pinch salt
1 cup sour cream (250 mL)
½ cup finely chopped walnuts (optional) (125 mL)

Cream butter and sugar until fluffy, add egg and vanilla. Blend in melted chocolate. Sift together the dry ingredients and add to the chocolate mixture alternately with the sour cream. Blend well. Stir in nuts if desired. Drop from a teaspoon onto a greased cookie sheet and bake at 350°F (180°C) for 10 minutes or until done. Remove from sheet, cool, then ice and store in sealed tin. They will keep fresh for about three days. Freeze if you prefer.

Chocolate Icing
3 cups icing sugar (750 mL)
¼ cup soft butter (50 mL)
3 tablespoon cocoa (45 mL)
2 tablespoons milk (30 mL)
1 tablespoon coffee liqueur or rum (15 mL)
1 teaspoon vanilla (5 mL)

Cream icing sugar and butter, add cocoa and liquids and beat until smooth and creamy. Ice the tops of all the cookies. (You may have more icing than you need.)

Blueberry Tart

A layer of blueberry custard is topped with a rich blueberry glaze. This two-layer tart is an elegant and delectable way to show off the beauty and taste of the Canadian blueberry.   Serves 8.

Pastry
> 1½ cups flour (375 mL)
> 3 tablespoons chilled shortening (45 mL)
> ½ cup chilled butter (125 mL)
> pinch salt
> 2 tablespoons sugar (30 mL)
> ⅓ cup cold water (75 mL)

To make pastry, combine flour, shortening, butter and salt in a bowl and work with pastry blender until mixture looks like small peas. Add cold water gradually until mixture forms a ball. Knead a little, wrap in wax paper and refrigerate until slightly chilled. Roll out and line a 9-inch (22 cm) tart or quiche pan.

Filling
> 2 cups blueberries, preferably fresh (500 mL)
> 3 tablespoons sugar (45 mL)
> 2 tablespoons rum, coffee or orange liqueur (30 mL)
> 1 tablespoon butter (15 mL)
> 3 tablespoons butter, softened (45 mL)
> ½ cup sugar (125 mL)
> 2 tablespoons cornstarch (30 mL)
> 3 large eggs
> ¼ cup whipping cream (50 mL)
> grated rind of 1 lemon
> 1 tablespoon lemon juice (15 mL)

To make filling, heat blueberries, sugar, liqueur and 1 tablespoon (15 mL) of butter in saucepan and stir to coat blueberries. Set aside. Beat remaining butter with sugar until light and fluffy. Add cornstarch, eggs and cream. Fold in lemon rind and juice, then fold into the berry mixture. Pour into tart shell and bake at 350°F (180°C) for about 30 minutes until set. Cool, then cover with glaze.

Glaze

1½ cups water (375 mL)
½ cup blueberries (125 mL)
1 cup white sugar (250 mL)
pinch cinnamon
pinch nutmeg
2 tablespoons lemon juice (30 mL)
4 tablespoons cornstarch (60 mL)
2 cups blueberries (500 mL)

To make glaze, mix water with ½ cup (125 mL) blueberries and bring to boil. Simmer for a few minutes, crush berries and strain juice. To the juice in another saucepan, add sugar, cinnamon, nutmeg and lemon juice, then gradually blend in the cornstarch. Bring to a boil and simmer until thick and clear. Fold in the 2 cups (500 mL) blueberries. Heat for about 5 minutes, then cool slightly and spread evenly over the cooked custard filling. Refrigerate overnight. You can decorate this with whipped cream or serve it with vanilla ice cream or sour cream but it's great just by itself.

If fresh blueberries are not available, use frozen ones. The effect is almost as good.

A Menu for All Seasons

Frozen Rum Daiquiri (page 22)
Crab Mousse
or
Hot Crab Delight
Liptauer Cheese tray (page 134)
Shrimp Istanbul
Chicken Breasts Supreme
Butter-Baked Rice
Vegetable Melange
Orange Mandarin Mould (page 156)
Breads — Olive, Cheese and Graham
Rum Cream Torte
Lemon Meringue Torte

This versatile menu makes a popular buffet presentation — the favourite of all my cooking school students. It needs no special season but is equally suitable for a family reunion, an Easter gathering or for entertaining friends on a summer evening. Whatever the occasion, this buffet will make it memorable. Simply by multiplying each recipe, from eight to 80 hungry guests can be satisfied, and children love it all. A bonus feature is that the entire meal can be prepared well in advance and is very easy to serve. You can relax and enjoy yourself, along with your guests.

Crab Mousse

Canned soup is the surprise ingredient. It gives the mousse a creamy consistency and a subtle flavour. Make it the day ahead.   Serves 16.

1 envelope unflavoured gelatin
3 tablespoons cold water (45 mL)
1 can cream of mushroom soup
6 ounces cream cheese, softened (180 gm)
¾ cup mayonnaise (200 mL)
½ cup chopped celery (125 mL)
4 tablespoons finely chopped green onion (60 mL)
⅛ teaspoon Dijon mustard (0.5 mL)
½ pound crab meat, fresh if possible (250 g)

Soften gelatin in cold water. Heat undiluted soup until hot, add gelatin and cream cheese and stir until creamy and smooth. Add all the rest of the ingredients and pour into an oiled 4-cup (1 L) mould and refrigerate overnight. Unmould on a bed of lettuce and garnish with parsley and lemon wedges. Serve with crackers.

Hot Crab Delight

This is a glorious appetizer, similar to a cheese fondue, and it can be made the night before serving. If you can't get fresh crabmeat, then substitute frozen or canned.   Serves 8 to 10.

12 ounces cream cheese (360 g)
1½ tablespoons milk or white wine (25 mL)
6 ounces crabmeat (180 g)
1 tablespoon finely chopped green onion (15 mL)
⅛ teaspoon Dijon mustard (0.5 mL)
toasted slivered almonds

Cream cheese with milk or wine until soft and smooth. Add crabmeat, onion and mustard and blend well. Place mixture in an oven-to-table dish and refrigerate overnight. Bake in a 350°F (180°C) oven for about 20 to 25 minutes or until hot and bubbly. Sprinkle with almonds during the last five minutes and serve with assorted crackers.

Shrimp Istanbul

This dish has been a lifesaver on many an occasion when friends arrive in town unexpectedly. With little time to prepare a special meal, this shrimp in a light and delicate sauce solves the problem. It takes only about 20 minutes to make. Serve with rice, sauteed pea pods or zucchini, a tossed green salad and a bottle of white wine — and you are ready to greet your guests. Serves 6 as main course, 10 for buffet.

4 tablespoons butter (60 mL)
1½ cups fresh mushrooms, sliced (375 mL)
1 medium onion, chopped
¾ to 1 pound fresh baby shrimp (375 to 500 g)
(frozen may be used)
4 tablespoons medium dry sherry (60 mL)
2 tablespoons tomato paste (30 mL)
1½ cups light cream (375 mL)
3½ tablespoons cornstarch (50 mL)
8 tablespoons light cream (125 mL)
½ cup sour cream (125 mL)

Saute onions and mushrooms in butter until slightly tender — about 3 minutes. Remove from pan and set aside. Add shrimp to same pan and saute for 2 minutes. Add sherry. Blend tomato paste with 1½ cups (375 mL) cream, then add to shrimp. Add cooked onions and mushrooms and simmer slowly for about 5 minutes. Blend together cornstarch and 8 tablespoons (125 mL) cream, add to shrimp mixture and stir gently, simmering, until mixture is thick. Fold in sour cream and turn into a 1½-quart (1.5 L) casserole. Refrigerate for up to 24 hours. Bake, covered, in a 350°F (180°C) oven for about 40 minutes or until hot. Remove cover for the final 10 minutes and stir until smooth. Serve over the rice.

Shrimp Istanbul freezes well. Remove from the freezer the night before serving and thaw in refrigerator. Sometimes freezing thins the sauce. If this happens, just add 1 tablespoon (15 mL) of cornstarch blended with a little cream. The sauce should be just thin enough to pour.

Chicken Breasts Supreme

An entree to remember! This is a simple yet elegant chicken recipe that appeals to everyone. Its unusual and subtle sour cream marinade contrasts a crisp outer coating. Serves 8 to 10.

6 chicken breasts (12 halves)
3 cups sour cream (750 mL)
juice of 1 lemon
½ teaspoon Worcestershire Sauce (2 mL)
½ teaspoon celery salt (2 mL)
¾ teaspoon Hungarian paprika (3 mL)
1 clove garlic, crushed
¼ teaspoon salt (1 mL)
pinch pepper
2½ cups fine dry breadcrumbs, approx. (625 mL)
¾ cup butter (200 mL)
¾ cup shortening (200 mL)

On the day before serving, cut each single chicken breast in half, making 24 pieces. Wipe with a cloth, debone and skin. Combine sour cream, lemon juice, Worcestershire Sauce, celery salt, paprika, garlic, salt and pepper in a large bowl. Add chicken pieces to sour cream mixture, coating each piece well, and let stand in bowl overnight, covered.

The next morning, remove chicken breasts one by one, leaving a good coating of sour cream on each, and coat well with bread crumbs. Arrange on a shallow greased cookie sheet, cover and refrigerate until ready to bake. Melt butter and shortening in saucepan and spoon about 2 teaspoons (10 mL) over each piece of chicken, enough to coat. Bake, uncovered, in preheated 350°F (180°C) oven for about 25 minutes. Spoon over the rest of the butter and bake for an additional 5 to 10 minutes until chicken is tender and still moist. Arrange on large platter, and decorate with orange slices, apple rings or thin wedges of peeled honeydew melon and cantaloupe.

This chicken is delicious cold for picnics or sandwiches.

Butter-Baked Rice

Beautifully seasoned with garlic and butter, this rice partners any meal. It can be made for any number of guests up to two days ahead of time. I usually make at least three times this recipe and tuck some away in the freezer for emergency occasions. It's great to have on hand for all dishes that call for cooked rice. I think that every student from my classes uses this recipe. Try it — you'll never have sticky rice again! Serves 6 at a buffet, 4 with main course.

> 1 cup long-grain rice (I use Uncle Ben's) (250 mL)
> boiling water
> ⅓ cup butter (75 mL)
> garlic salt
> 1¾ cups chicken stock (450 mL)
> chopped parsley
> toasted slivered almonds
> paprika

Place rice in casserole or saucepan and add enough boiling water to cover rice by about 5 inches (12 cm). Let stand for 30 or 40 minutes, then strain and rinse well with cold water until all starch is removed. Drain rice well. Melt butter in heavy casserole or Dutch oven. Add rice and cook over medium heat, stirring frequently, until rice has absorbed all the butter — about 5 minutes. Sprinkle with garlic salt and add chicken stock. Cover and refrigerate for up to 2 days.

   Pre-heat oven to 375°F (190°C) (or 350°F (180°C) if you are cooking other foods at this temperature at the same time). Give the rice a stir, cover well with foil under the lid and bake for about 1½ hours or until all stock is absorbed. (Add 20 minutes if at 350°F (180°C).) Sprinkle rice with chopped parsley, paprika and toasted slivered almonds. (To toast almonds, place on cookie sheet and bake at 350°F (180°C) for 6 to 8 minutes until golden.)

Vegetable Melange

This colourful and easy salad platter gets a head start the night before serving and the tangy salad dressing can be made days ahead. Vegetable substitutions can be made but try to include the hearts of palm and artichokes for they give a special touch and taste. It is great for barbecue parties or as a meal in itself with a pound of marinated fresh baby shrimp in the centre of the platter.

> 1 14-ounce can hearts of palm (398 mL), sliced ¼-inch (6 mm) thick
> 1 14-ounce can artichoke hearts, drained (398 mL)
> 2 14-ounce (398 mL) cans green asparagus, drained
>   or fresh, cooked slightly
> 1 14-ounce can white asparagus, drained (398 mL)
> 5 celery stalks, sliced on the diagonal
> 20 cherry tomatoes
>   or 6 large tomatoes, thickly sliced
> butter or romaine lettuce
> 2 large avocados, peeled and sliced
> pimiento strips
> green and black olives
> chopped green onion
> 1 cooked egg yolk
> vinaigrette dressing (see below)

Marinate in separate bowls in vinaigrette dressing the hearts of palm, artichokes (cut in half if large), asparagus, celery and tomatoes. Cover and refrigerate. Slice avocado just before serving and dip slices in lemon juice to prevent darkening. Arrange drained vegetables on platter spread with lettuce, alternating the colours of red, white and green. Sprinkle tomatoes with green onion; press egg yolk through a sieve over the asparagus and decorate with pimiento strips. Alternate green and black olives around the platter rim.

Vinaigrette Dressing

¾ cup salad oil (200 mL)
¼ cup white wine vinegar (50 mL)
1 tablespoon lemon juice (15 mL)
pinches of sweet basil, oregano and chervil
1 clove garlic, crushed
1 egg yolk
¼ teaspoon Maggi seasoning (1 mL)
salt and pepper
¼ teaspoon Dijon mustard
  or dry mustard (1 mL)

Combine all in a jar, shake well, and store, covered, in refrigerator for a few days. Add more or less vinegar and lemon juice depending on how tart you like the dressing. I usually triple this recipe to make sure I have enough for the marinade.

This recipe makes a good all-round salad dressing for any kind of mixed green salad.

Breads

These three moist breads are quick to make, do not require yeast and never fail. They are served at room temperature so no last minute heating is required. Just slice thinly, spread with butter and arrange in rows on a platter. All three varieties freeze well.

Graham Bread

2 tablespoons brown sugar (30 mL)
½ teaspoon baking soda (1 mL)
1 tablespoon baking powder (15 mL)
½ teaspoon salt (2 mL)
⅓ cup skim milk powder (75 mL)
1 cup all-purpose flour (250 mL)
2 cups graham flour (500 mL)
1¾ cups water (425 mL)

Combine all ingredients except water, stirring to blend well. Add water and stir just to mix. Well grease a clean 2-pound (1 kg) tin (juice or shortening tins are fine) and pour in bread mix. Seal top with greased aluminum foil. Bake in 350°F (180°C) oven for 1½ hours. Do not peek! Remove from can immediately when done, cool and wrap in foil. Slice paper thin to serve. This is great as the base for open-faced sandwiches of shaved ham and mustard relish or toasted with home-made jam.

Quick Cheddar Cheese Bread

   2 cups flour (500 mL)
   4 teaspoons baking powder (20 mL)
   ¼ teaspoon salt (1 mL)
   ¼ cup butter (50 mL)
   1 cup grated medium Cheddar cheese (250 mL)
   2 eggs
   ¼ cup white sugar (50 mL)
   1 cup milk (250 mL)

Sift flour, baking powder and salt and cut in butter until mixture resembles small peas. Add cheese and toss. Beat eggs until fluffy, gradually add sugar then milk and add to dry ingredients. Blend just to combine. Pour into 8 by 4-inch (20 x 10 cm) loaf pan and bake at 350°F (180°C) for 50 to 60 minutes or until it tests done with a straw. Remove from pan and cool. This bread can be served hot or cold, sliced thinly.

Olive Bread

   2 eggs
   1 tablespoon sugar (15 mL)
   ½ teaspoon salt (2 mL)
   2 tablespoons olive oil (30 mL)
   ¾ cup chopped black olives (200 mL)
   2 cups flour (500 mL)
   2 teaspoons baking powder (10 mL)
   1 cup milk (250 mL)

Beat eggs lightly and stir in sugar, salt, oil and olives. Stir in flour, baking powder and milk. Don't beat, just blend to mix. Pour into well-greased 8 by 4-inch (20 x 10 cm) bread pan and bake at 350°F (180°C) for 45 to 55 minutes or until done. This loaf does not rise as high as other breads but it is delicious, especially with Cheddar and German butter cheese.

Rum Cream Torte

This torte always bring compliments — and requests for the recipe. I usually tuck several in my freezer for unexpected company for it makes a refreshing ending to any meal, especially during Christmas.
Serves 12 to 16.

Crust
> 1 package chocolate wafers crushed
> (should yield 2 cups) (500 mL)
> ½ cup melted butter (125 mL)

Filling
> 1 package unflavoured gelatin
> ¼ cup cold water (50 mL)
> ⅓ cup white rum (75 mL)
> 6 egg yolks
> 1 cup white sugar (250 mL)
> 1 pint whipping cream, whipped (500 mL)

Garnish
> kiwi fruit, peeled and sliced
> mandarin oranges, drained
> maraschino cherries, halved

Combine wafers and butter and press on bottom and sides of a 9-inch (22 cm) springform pan. Soak gelatin in water, bring to a slight boil to dissolve then cool slightly. Add rum and set aside. Beat egg yolks until thick, then slowly add sugar, beating constantly. Fold in the cool gelatin mixture, then gently fold in the whipped cream. Pour into wafer-lined pan, wrap well and freeze. This can be made weeks ahead and will keep in the freezer for several months. It can be served frozen or as a refrigerated rum mousse. To serve, remove from pan and decorate with fruit. This recipe makes enough filling for three 8-inch (20 cm) pies if you prefer.

Lemon Meringue Torte

This recipe comes from sister-in-law Ruth in Halifax. It is as smooth as velvet and makes a nice, tart ending to any meal. It can be made days or weeks ahead. Half of this recipe will fill a 9-inch (22 cm) pie. For variety, substitute limeade for the lemonade, or use a combination of both.

Serves 16.

Crust

> 3 cups vanilla wafer crumbs
>   or digestive biscuit crumbs (750 mL)
> ½ cup melted butter (125 mL)

Filling

> 6 large eggs, separated
> 2 14-ounce (398 mL) cans sweetened condensed milk
> 1 12½-ounce can frozen lemonade, thawed (355 mL)
> 1 pint whipping cream, whipped (500 mL)
> ¾ cup sugar (200 mL)

Combine wafer crumbs and butter and press into a foil-lined 13 by 9-inch (22 x 33 cm) pan. Bake in 350°F (180°C) oven for about 7 minutes. Cool. Beat egg yolks, add condensed milk and lemonade (undiluted), and fold in the whipped cream. Pour into cooled crust. Beat egg whites until foamy, beat in sugar 1 tablespoon (15 mL) at a time and continue beating until stiff. Spread over the filling. Put under the broiler, 4 inches (10 cm) from the heat, and brown lightly. This takes just seconds so don't turn your back. Cover pan without crushing meringue and seal well with foil. Wrap and store in freezer. Remove from freezer about 20 to 25 minutes before serving to soften slightly. Transfer from pan and decorate with lime and lemon slices and fresh strawberries. Cut into 2-inch (5 cm) squares to serve.

Greek with Gusto

Hummus
Tsatziki (page 97)
Dolmathes
Pita Bread
Greek Salad (page 99)
Tomatoes with Feta Cheese
Chicken a la Grecque
Garides me Saltsa
(Shrimp in Feta Cheese)
Butter-baked Rice with Pine Nuts (page 74)
Red Snapper en Papillote
Grand Marnier Cake
Fresh Fruit in Sauterne
Chablis, Reisling or a hearty red Beaujolais

The flamboyant cuisine of Greece has become increasingly popular and this buffet menu will satisfy any aficionado. Three entrees are included and you may use one or all, depending on the number of guests. Freshly caught lobsters, prawns, red snapper and other fish play their part in traditional Greek food and lamb and chicken are often wrapped in delectable thin pastry sheets known as filo paper. Fresh fruits and vegetables add texture and colour, with feta cheese and pine nuts for accent along with herbs and spices such as mint, oregano, basil, rosemary and dill. Most specialty shops or gourmet food sections will have a good selection of authentic ingredients.

Hummus

An interesting dish of cooked, pureed chick peas blended to the consistency of thick mayonnaise, hummus is traditionally served along with the cucumber Tsatziki, with pita bread, the flat, hollow loaves of Armenia and Syria.   Serves 8.

1 14-ounce can chick peas (garbanzo beans) (398 mL)
½ to ¾ cup olive oil (125 to 200 mL)
juice of half a lemon, or to taste
¼ cup prepared tahini (sesame) paste (50 mL)
1 clove garlic, crushed
salt and pepper to taste

Drain chick peas and rinse with cold water. In a blender or food processor puree chick peas, then add oil, lemon juice, tahini paste, garlic, salt and pepper. Add oil gradually; if the mixture seems dry, increase the amount of oil. The hummus should be creamy like a dip. It can be made the day ahead of serving and stored in the refrigerator. Moisten with olive oil if it dries out. (Tahini paste can be obtained from specialty or health food store.)

Dolmathes

These are grape leaves stuffed with a rice filling and pickled. They are readily available from Greek food stores or delicatessens. Allow two dolmathes per person and heat at 350°F (180°C) for about 25 minutes. Decorate with slices of lemon and strips of pimento.

Tomatoes with Feta Cheese

These stuffed cherry tomatoes make tasty appetizers and add colour to the rice pilaf. For a side salad, use regular-sized tomatoes, cut in half, then stuffed.   Serves 8 to 10

> 25 to 30 firm cherry tomatoes
> 4 tablespoons chopped green onion (60 mL)
> ¾ cup crumbled feta cheese (200 mL)
> pinches of basil and oregano
> salt and pepper
> 1 tablespoon olive oil (15 mL)
> 1 teaspoon fresh lemon juice (5 mL)
> ripe olives, diced

Cut the tops off the tomatoes, scoop out the pulp and set aside, discarding the seeds. Slice a very thin piece off the bottoms of the tomatoes so they will sit steadily. Chop the pulp, add onions, cheese, herbs and seasoning and blend with oil and lemon juice. Add more oil if filling is too dry. Stuff each tomato with the mixture and decorate each with a piece of olive. Refrigerate until ready to serve.

If using this recipe for a side salad, choose medium tomatoes and prepare as above, serving each half on a bed of leafy lettuce. This would be nice with a quiche for a light luncheon.

Chicken a la Grecque

Chicken pieces bathed in a subtle lemon sauce are baked between crispy sheets of filo paper. These pastry sheets, commonly used in many Greek recipes, can be obtained in specialty stores, usually in the frozen food section. Thaw according to directions on the package and keep the sheets covered with clear plastic wrap while you work to prevent them from drying out. With a bit of practice, you'll find filo paper is fun to work with and gratifying to serve. This dish can be prepared the day ahead of serving and it makes a light dinner in itself, along with a Greek salad, tsatziki and bread.   Serves 8.

1 onion, chopped
½ cup chopped celery (125 mL)
1 clove garlic, crushed
4 cups diced, cooked chicken or turkey (1 L)
7 tablespoons butter (105 mL)
5 tablespoons flour (75 mL)
2 cups chicken stock (500 mL)
6 eggs
¼ cup parsley, chopped (50 mL)
1 tablespoon dill (15 mL)
juice of half a lemon
pinch nutmeg
salt and pepper
18 sheets filo paper
melted butter

Saute onion, celery and garlic in 3 tablespoons (45 mL) butter for about three minutes. Add to the chicken in a bowl. (If you don't have leftover chicken, bake 8 chicken breasts in foil for 30 minutes at 325°F (160°C) until tender; cool, remove skin and bones and dice into ½-inch (1 cm) cubes.) Melt the remaining 4 tablespoons (60 mL) butter in a skillet, add flour and mix over low heat for about three minutes; do not brown. Whisk in the chicken stock gradually and cook over medium heat until boiling, stirring constantly. Continue cooking and stirring for three minutes until sauce is thick. Reduce heat and simmer for 5 minutes.

Beat eggs just until blended. Slowly pour one cup of the hot sauce into the eggs, then stir the egg mixture into the remaining sauce. Return to the heat and stir well; remove just as it reaches the boiling point. If you let it boil, the sauce will curdle. (If it does, beat it rapidly with a wire whisk until smooth.) Add parsley, dill, lemon juice, nutmeg, salt and pepper, then fold in the chicken mixture.

Brush both sides of one sheet of filo paper with melted butter and press onto the bottom and sides of a 13 x 9 x 3-inch (33 x 22 x 5 cm) baking pan. Repeat with eight more sheets of filo and spoon cold chicken mixture over. Top with nine more layers of filo, each one buttered lightly on both sides. Cover well and refrigerate until ready to bake. Heat oven to 375°F (190°C) and bake uncovered for about 35 to 40 minutes until golden and bubbly. Let dish stand for five minutes, then cut into squares.

Garides Me Saltsa

You will often see this shrimp dish as an appetizer on a Greek restaurant menu but I prefer to serve it as a main course over rice. The shrimp simmers slowly in a tomato, wine and feta cheese sauce with just a hint of garlic. Fresh shrimp is best, though frozen is satisfactory.   Serves 8.

1 tablespoon olive oil (15 mL)
1 tablespoon butter (15 mL)
½ cup finely chopped onion (125 mL)
½ green pepper, seeded and chopped
1 small clove garlic, crushed
1 28-ounce can whole tomatoes, chopped (796 mL)
   or 8 to 10 fresh tomatoes, peeled and chopped
½ cup dry white wine (125 mL)
¼ cup dry white wine (50 mL)
4 tablespoons finely chopped parsley (60 mL)
½ teaspoon oregano (2 mL)
½ teaspoon basil (2 mL)
¼ teaspoon cumin (1 mL)
pepper
¾ to 1 pound cooked baby shrimp (375 to 500 g)
8 ounces feta cheese, crumbled (250 g)

In a heavy frying pan, heat oil and butter over medium heat and saute onions, green pepper and garlic until soft but not brown. Add tomatoes, ½ cup wine (125 mL), half the parsley, herbs and seasoning. Simmer until sauce thickens — about 30 to 40 minutes. Add shrimp, cover and refrigerate overnight in a large shallow casserole dish. The following day, add the ¼ cup (50 mL) wine, sprinkle with feta cheese and bake at 375°F (190°C) for about 35 to 40 minutes until hot and bubbly. Sprinkle with remaining parsley and serve over rice.

Fresh prawns may be substituted. Saute prawns in their shells in 2 tablespoons (30 mL) olive oil until they begin to curl. Remove from heat, cool, remove shells and stir into hot sauce. Crumble feta cheese on top and bake for 10 minutes at 350°F (180°C) or until cheese melts.

Red Snapper en Papillote

The parchment paper for this dish may be obtained at a kitchen specialty shop, but heavy aluminum foil may be used instead. The paper seals in the juices and the flavour, making the fish succulent.   Serves 8.

1 red snapper, about 4 to 4½ pounds (2 to 2.25 kg)
olive oil
pepper
4 lemons, thinly sliced
oregano
1 pound large fresh shrimp or prawn (in shells) (500 g)

Ask your fishmonger to remove the bones from the fish, leaving the head and tail intact. Rub the cavity with a little of the olive oil and season with pepper. Arrange 6 lemon slices inside. Brush two 24-inch (.6 m) pieces of parchment, large enough to hold the fish, with olive oil. Place sheets crosswise on a large cookie sheet and place 6 more lemon slices on top. Place fish on top of the lemons, drizzle with 3 to 4 tablespoons (45 to 60 mL) oil, sprinkle with oregano and pepper and arrange shrimp around fish. Place remaining lemon slices on top and wrap fish in the paper, tying the ends with string and sealing the fold with paper clips. Bake at 400°F (200°C) for about 30 minutes or until done. Transfer wrapped fish to serving platter, break open paper along the centre and roll back edges. Serve with the juices as sauce and shrimp and lemons as garnish.

The red snapper, surrounded by shrimps and lemon slices, sits on a bed of parchment.

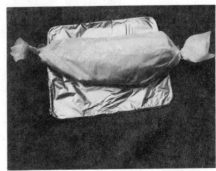

The fish is then wrapped securely and ready for the oven. The parchment keeps the fish juicy.

Grand Marnier Cake

This moist cake is similar in texture to a pound cake. Serve it in summer with fresh strawberries or instead of fruitcake during the Christmas season. It freezes well.

Serves 8 to 10.

1 cup butter (250 mL)
1 cup white sugar (250 mL)
4 eggs, separated
4 tablespoons Grand Marnier (60 mL)
2 cups white flour (500 mL)
1 teaspoon baking powder (5 mL)
1 teaspoon baking soda (5 mL)
1 cup sour cream (250 mL)
grated rind of 1 orange
6 ounces of pecans, chopped (180 g)
½ cup golden raisins, chopped (125 mL)
slivered almonds, toasted

Glaze
1 cup white sugar (250 mL)
1 cup orange juice (250 mL)
⅔ cup Grand Marnier (150 mL)

Cream butter and sugar until light and fluffy. Add egg yolks, one at a time, beating well, then add Grand Marnier. Sift dry ingredients together and add to the batter alternately with the sour cream, ending with the dry ingredients. Add rind, nuts and raisins. Beat egg whites until stiff, then gently fold into the batter. Pour into a greased 9-inch (22 cm) bundt or angel food pan and bake at 350°F (180°C) for 50 to 55 minutes or until done. Cool slightly and remove from pan.

Combine ingredients for glaze in saucepan and cook to the soft ball stage (235°F (110°C) on a candy thermometre). Puncture warm cake all over with a skewer, then spoon hot glaze evenly over the top and sides. Cool, then stud with toasted slivered almonds. Store in airtight cake tin or freeze.

Après Ski Spectacular

Hot Mulled Wine
Cheese Fondue
or
Crudites of Vegetables with Herbed Dip
or
Kippered Salmon with Crackers
Sauteed Zucchini Strips
Assorted Cheeses
Cassoulet Francais
Salad Deluxe
Wholewheat Loaf
Amaretto Cheesecake
Sambuca

This is a dinner that hungry skiers will rush off the mountain for. It starts with an assortment of appetizers and a mug or two of mulled wine — a great way to relax around a cosy fire while the main course, a hearty cassoulet, bubbles in the oven. Good bread and a salad and the meal's complete, except of course, for dessert, a luscious cheesecake. The menu sounds ambitious for a ski cabin but all the food preparation can be done in advance then transported to your mountain retreat. Just make sure that you're back from the slopes by 3:30 to put the cassoulet in the oven and to do the last minute fixings.

Our après ski party was held at Whistler for a crew of 16. The skiing was great — the eating sensational!

Mulled Wine

The addition of fruit juices make this version extra smooth and refreshing.   Serves 6.

   4 cups Burgundy (1 L)
   2 cups apple juice (500 mL)
   2 cups pineapple juice (500 mL)
   1 cup cranberry juice (250 mL)
   4 tablespoons brown sugar (60 mL)
   ½ tablespoon cinnamon (7 mL)
   ¼ tablespoon cloves (3 mL)

Mix all together, heat slowly and serve steaming hot. Add a cinnamon stick to each mug.

Cheese Fondue

Everyone has their own version of this classic cheese dish but this is the one that I prefer. Cook it over low heat (don't overcook it or the cheese will become stringy) and keep it hot for serving over a sterno heater or candle. For guaranteed success, use only imported Swiss cheese.
                                                                    Serves 8.

   1 clove garlic
   2 cups dry white wine (500 mL)
   1 pound imported Swiss cheese, Gruyere or Emmentaler
      or a mixture (500 g)
   3 tablespoons flour (45 mL)
   salt and pepper to taste
   pinch of nutmeg
   6 tablespoons kirsch
      or 6 additional tablespoons wine (90 mL)
   1 large loaf of French bread, cut into
      one-inch (2.5 cm) cubes (crust on each)

Peel garlic and rub it over the bottom of chafing dish or casserole. Pour in the wine and heat very slowly. Mix cheeses with flour and when wine starts to bubble, add cheese mixture in small handfuls to the pot, stirring with a fork until the cheese is melted before adding another handful. When fondue is smooth and starts to bubble, season to taste and add nutmeg. Slowly pour in kirsch or extra wine and blend well.

To serve: Spear bread with fondue fork, going through the soft part first and securing the points in the crust. This way you are less likely to lose the bread. If fondue becomes too thick, pour in a little warm white wine and blend.

Crudites of Vegetables with Herbed Dip

Choose an assortment of four or five of the following vegetables. Most can be prepared the night before and kept fresh in the refrigerator. Zucchini, carrots, celery, cucumber, cut into finger-length sticks; cherry tomatoes; cauliflower in small chunks; broccoli flowerets; medium-size mushrooms, cleaned.

A few hours before serving, arrange romaine lettuce on a large platter; place bowl of dip in middle and place the vegetables in clusters on top of the lettuce.

Herbed Dip

The hint of curry gives this dip a real lift. You can make this two to three days ahead of time and refrigerate. It is everyone's favourite.

Makes about 3½ cups (875 mL).

2 cups mayonnaise (500 mL)
⅔ cup plain yogurt (150 mL)
1 cup sour cream (250 mL)
2 tablespoons dill weed, or to taste (30 mL)
½ teaspoon chervil (2 mL)
¼ teaspoon Dijon mustard (1 mL)
⅛ teaspoon curry powder (0.5 mL)
½ teaspoon lemon juice (2 mL)
salt and pepper

Combine everything and mix well. This dip is also great with potato chips and if you add four or five tablespoons of salad oil to the recipe it becomes a tasty salad dressing.

Kippered Salmon

This smoked fish is available in large chunks at most seafood markets. Cut it into small cubes and serve with crackers and a sauce made from mayonnaise, a dash of lemon juice and a little dill weed.

Sauteed Zucchini Strips

Deep-fried zucchini strips have become popular for appetizers but I prefer to saute them in butter. They can be made the day ahead then reheated in the oven but they are at their best when cooked minutes before serving.   Serves 8 to 10 for appetizers

> 3 medium zucchini
> salt and pepper
> flour
> 3 eggs
> 3 tablespoons milk (45 mL)
> 2 cups cracker crumbs (500 mL)
> ½ cup grated Parmesan cheese (125 mL)
> butter
> lemon juice

Cut zucchini into strips about ⅓ inch wide (1 cm) and 3 inches (7 cm) long. Sprinkle with salt and pepper, pat dry, then roll in flour. Beat eggs and milk and combine cracker crumbs and Parmesan cheese. Dip zucchini first into egg mixture, then roll in crumbs to coat well. Heat enough butter to fill fry pan to ¼ inch (6 mm) level and saute zucchini until lightly brown and crisp — about 5 minutes. Sprinkle with lemon juice and serve immediately. If zucchini are large, you might need more coating. Keep frypan well supplied with butter for each batch — the coating soaks it up. To reheat, place zucchini strips on cookie sheet and heat for 5 minutes in a 350°F (180°C) oven.

Cassoulet Francais

This must be the world's most sumptuous version of baked beans. I have simplified the original recipe so that it can be assembled two days ahead of serving. Feeds 20 generously.

The Beans

16 cups chicken stock (4 L)
    or dissolve 12 chicken cubes in hot water
6 cups dry small white beans (1.5 L)
1 5½-ounce can tomato paste (156 mL)
1 large clove garlic, crushed
¼ teaspoon basil (1 mL)
¼ teaspoon thyme (1 mL)
pepper

Two days ahead of serving, bring chicken stock to boil in a large heavy casserole. Drop in the beans, cover and simmer for about 1½ to 2 hours until just tender. Don't overcook — the beans will be mushy. Remove to a large bowl, drain and reserve the stock. You should have about 9 cups (2.25 L) of stock; if short, add more chicken stock to make up the difference. Add tomato paste, garlic, herbs and pepper. Put stock mixture into a container, seal and refrigerate. Refrigerate the beans separately.

The Meat

¾ pound salt pork, cut into small cubes (375 g)
1 medium onion, chopped
3¼ pounds pork butt (1.5 kg), trimmed of fat
    and cut into 1½-inch (4 cm) cubes
20 chicken thighs, skinned
1 pound non-garlic pork sausage (500 g)

Rinse salt pork well to remove excess salt then saute in large skillet with the onion until golden. Set aside. Put a little salad oil into same skillet and saute pork cubes until browned. Set aside with salt pork. Add more oil to pan and brown chicken thighs. Set aside. Slice sausage into thin slices; set aside.

In large casserole place a thin layer of beans, arrange a third of the pork sausage on top, then a third of the salt pork mixture and a third of the chicken thighs. Repeat these layers twice more, ending with a layer of beans. There should be four layers of beans and three layers of the meats. Cover and refrigerate.

About 3 to 3½ hours before serving, pour reserved chicken stock over the bean mixture in the casserole until the stock just covers the beans. Cover and bake for 2 hours. Sprinkle top with the following mixture: 1½ cups (375 mL) fine bread crumbs blended with 4 tablespoons (60 mL) butter. Bake uncovered for about one more hour or until cassoulet is thick, bubbly and still slightly moist on the inside. Sprinkle with chopped parsley and serve triumphantly. Bake at 350°F (180°C)

Check the cassoulet after 2½ hours to see if it is thickened but still moist. If it looks a little dry, add more stock. If you are cooking only half quantities, bake only for 1½ hours covered, then sprinkle with crumb mixture and bake for 1 more hour. Check on its progress after 40 minutes. To serve leftovers the next day, you may need to add more stock or tomato juice. Leftovers can also be frozen. For the second time around, I add some baked or fried chicken to the meal, or serve the cassoulet with hamburgers.

Salad Deluxe

This salad goes together in layers, chills for several hours to mellow before serving and makes its own dressing in the process. It is my most popular salad, especially with the men. Serves 8 but is easy to multiply.

3 to 4 heads of lettuce, cleaned
1 cup mayonnaise, approx. (250 mL)
1 sweet white onion, thinly sliced
sugar
salt and pepper
1 cup processed Swiss cheese, in julienne strips (250 mL)
1½ cups slightly cooked green peas (375 mL)
½ pound bacon, fried crisp and crumbled (250 g)

In a large salad bowl place a third of the lettuce and dot with several spoonfuls of mayonnaise. Top with a third of the onion slices, sprinkle with sugar (about 2 teaspoons (10 mL) in every layer) and add a dash of salt and pepper. Add a third of the peas and cheese in an even layer. Repeat layers, ending with lettuce. Cover with plastic wrap to seal well and refrigerate. Do not toss. Just before serving, add bacon and toss gently.

Wholewheat Loaf

This bread never fails and is tasty, hearty and wholesome. It is best made on the day of serving and eaten while still warm. If you make it in the morning, simply reheat at 350°F (180°C) for ten minutes. The bread can also be frozen. Thaw it overnight and reheat. Makes one loaf.

Serves 6 to 8.

2 cups wholewheat flour (500 mL)
2 cups white all-purpose flour (500 mL)
2 teaspoons double acting baking powder (10 mL)
1 teaspoon salt (5 mL)
1 teaspoon baking soda (5 mL)
2 tablespoons brown sugar (30 mL)
1 egg, beaten
2 cups buttermilk (500 mL)
large oatmeal flakes

Combine dry ingredients in a large bowl. Mix the egg with the butter-milk and mix with dry ingredients. Dust board with oatmeal flakes, turn out dough and knead about 10 times to cover with flakes and form a round ball. Cut a cross lightly on top of the loaf, place on buttered cookie sheet and bake at 375°F (190°C) for about 45 to 50 minutes or until it sounds hollow.

When ready to serve, place loaf on a wooden platter and let guests cut their own slices. Provide soft butter blended with a little chopped green onion and chopped parsley. This bread is also excellent with cheese.

Amaretto Cheesecake

My daughter Jennifer's favourite dessert is our family cheesecake. It is simple to whip up and looks gorgeous served with fresh strawberries or kiwi fruit or with sliced peaches marinated in Amaretto. If you don't like Amaretto, or for a change, substitute another liqueur or use 1 teaspoon vanilla essence in both filling and topping.   Serves 10 to 12.

Crust
1½ cups finely ground vanilla wafer crumbs (375 mL)
¾ cup finely ground hazelnuts, pecans or almonds (200 mL)
2 tablespoons brown sugar (30 mL)
4 tablespoons butter, melted (60 mL)

Filling
24 ounces cream cheese (750 g)
1 cup white sugar (250 mL)
4 eggs
3 tablespoons Amaretto (45 mL)

Topping
1 pint sour cream (500 mL)
3 tablespoons sugar (45 mL)
2 tablespoons Amaretto (30 mL)
additional nuts, toasted, for garnish

In bowl, combine crumbs, nuts, sugar and butter. Pat the mixture onto the bottom and sides of a 8-inch (20 cm) springform pan or divide between two 8-inch (20 cm) pie plates if you prefer. (The smaller sizes are great for tucking away in the freezer.) Refrigerate.

Heat oven to 350°F (180°C). In a mixing bowl, cream the cheese and gradually beat in the sugar. Add eggs and liqueur and blend until smooth. Pour into crust and bake until set — about 45 minutes. Do not overcook; the filling should just be firm. Set aside to cool while you make the topping. Combine sour cream, sugar and Amaretto and spread evenly over cheesecake. Bake for another 5 minutes. Cool, then refrigerate or freeze. This can be made a day or two ahead.

Sambuca

An interesting liqueur from Italy, Sambuca is made from elderberries and green aniseed. Serve it in small heatproof liqueur glasses with three roasted coffee beans in each. Set the Sambuca aflame to let the coffee beans release their aroma.

A Menu for all Seasons, page 70, photographed at the home of Haik Gharibian.
Overleaf, Picnic in the Park, page 63, left. Right, Greek with Gusto, page 80, photographed at the home of John and Sharon Woyat.

Fitness Feast

Jogger's Special
Artichoke Frittata
Crudités of Vegetables
Tzatziki Sauce
Wholewheat Pita Bread
Chicken in Filo
Brown Rice Pilaf
Greek Salad
Carrot Cake
Diane's Health Cookies
Ambrosia Cake
Fresh Fruit Platter
White Chenin Blanc

A fitness feast? Ridiculous! The two are incompatible. That may be your first reaction but not all fit people are on the carrot sticks and bean sprouts regime. Most like to eat and eat well, and can do so without jeopardizing their fitness quotient. Fitness and good food are natural companions. This menu will satisfy the appetites of a crew of hungry friends just back from a jog round Stanley Park, a game of tennis, a six-hour hike — or whatever sports activity turns you on.

Jogger's Special

I like to serve this drink at a special brunch with friends after our Sunday morning run.   Serves 10.

4 cups fresh orange juice (1 L)
   or frozen juice, diluted
1 bottle Champagne or sparkling white wine
1 cup Perrier water (250 mL)

Chill everything well. Combine at the last minute and serve in champagne glasses or wine goblets.

Apres Ski Spectacular, page 87, photographed at the Whistler cabin f Ross and Linda Davidson.

Crudités of Vegetables

Raw vegetables are always popular (as well as healthy) and they look so colourful, especially when they are arranged like a bouquet of flowers in a basket made of bread dough. The basket used in the photograph was made for me by a local bakery but it would be fun to make one yourself. Fill basket with styrofoam cubes, cover foam with leafy lettuce, impale raw vegetable "flowers" on Chinese bamboo skewers and pierce skewers through the styrofoam. Use three different sizes of skewers for a well-balanced arrangement.

I used cherry tomatoes; the white tips of green onions, fringed; radish roses; green and black olives; carrot and parsnip rings, scalloped; zucchini; celery; etc.

Guests help themselves to the bouquet, and dip the vegetables in Tzatziki or other herbed dip.

Tzatziki

This is my version of the popular Greek cucumber appetizer. Serve it as a dip with the raw vegetables and pita bread. It is also a good companion for the chicken in filo paper as well as lamb. Makes about 2½ cups (625 mL) to serve 8 to 10.

> 1 large English cucumber, chopped finely
>   or 1 regular cucumber, peeled, seeded and chopped
> salt
> 1½ cups plain yogurt (375 mL)
> ½ cup sour cream (125 mL)
> 1 small clove garlic, crushed
> 3 teaspoons chopped green onion (15 mL)
> 1 teaspoon lemon juice (5 mL)
> ½ teaspoon white wine vinegar (2 mL)
> pinch pepper
> 2 teaspoons dill weed (10 mL)
> ¼ teaspoon Dijon mustard (1 mL)

Sprinkle cucumber with salt, place on paper towels and let stand for 10 minutes. Pat dry. Mix rest of ingredients, fold in the cucumber, adding more or less lemon juice or vinegar to taste. Refrigerate, covered, for 2 to 3 days.

Artichoke Frittata

This appetizer always brings comment. It can be made the day ahead, then reheated at 350°F (180°C) for about 10 to 15 minutes before serving. A frittata is similar to a quiche but doesn't have a crust.   Serves 8.

3 6½-ounce (184 mL) jars marinated artichokes
½ pound medium Cheddar cheese, grated (250 g)
1 small onion, finely chopped
4 large eggs, lightly beaten
6 single soda crackers, crushed
dash of Tabasco (optional)
salt and pepper

Drain artichokes and chop into small pieces. Mix with all the rest of the ingredients and pour into a buttered 8 or 9-inch (20 or 22 cm) quiche or pie pan. Bake in pre-heated 325°F (160°C) oven for 35 to 40 minutes or until a knife inserted into the centre comes out clean. Cut into 1-inch (2.5 cm) squares and serve warm.

Chicken in Filo Paper

These chicken breasts stuffed with fresh spinach, feta cheese and dill and wrapped in filo paper are winners at any party. They can be prepared a day ahead if necessary, then baked just before serving. Allow 1½ chicken breasts per person.

single chicken breasts, boned, skinned and halved
fresh spinach leaves, washed and dried
dill weed
feta cheese
filo paper
melted butter, lukewarm

Keep butter slightly warm in saucepan and get filo paper ready, covered with plastic wrap to prevent it drying out. Brush one sheet very slightly on both sides with the melted butter. (I dampen my hands with a little butter and smear them gently over the paper.) Cut the sheet lengthwise into 3-inch (7.5 cm) strips. Place a piece of chicken on the lower corner of one of the strips, cover with 1 or 2 fresh spinach leaves, sprinkle over about 1 teaspoon (5 mL) of feta cheese and dill to taste and place another spinach leaf on top. Fold filo paper over the filling, enclosing it from side to side, right to left, lengthwise to form a triangular package. Continue to stuff and wrap all the chicken pieces in the same manner and place them on a greased cookie sheet. Brush with a little more butter if the pastry starts to dry out. (At this point, the chicken packages can be refrigerated; wrap well.)

Bake chicken, uncovered, in pre-heated 375°F (190°C) oven for 20 to 25 minutes until golden. Don't overcook — the chicken should be moist and the filo crisp. Use two sheets of filo for a thicker wrapping, if desired.

Brown Rice Pilaf

The nut-like flavour of the brown rice and the colourful vegetables make this casserole a perfect match for lamb as well as chicken. As a bonus, its nutritional value is high.   Serves 6.

> 3 cups chicken broth (750 mL)
> ½ teaspoon basil (2 mL)
> 1 teaspoon dry dill weed (5 mL)
> 1 cup brown rice, uncooked (250 mL)
>   (I use Uncle Ben's)
> 1 small onion, sliced
> 1 clove garlic, pressed
> ½ green pepper, seeded and finely chopped
> ½ cup fresh mushrooms, sliced (125 mL)
> 1 tomato, peeled, seeded and cubed

In a saucepan combine broth, basil, dill, thyme and rice. Cover and cook for about 50 to 60 minutes or until stock is all absorbed. Saute all vegetables except for the tomato separately until tender. Blend vegetables with cooked rice, add tomato and turn into baking dish. Cover and refrigerate for up to 24 hours. Bake, covered, for about 30 minutes in a 350°F or 375°F (180 or 190°C) oven. If desired, uncover the casserole for the last 10 minutes, sprinkle with about ½ cup (125 mL) of Monterey Jack or Mozzarella cheese and bake until cheese melts.

Greek Salad

This salad can be assembled ahead of time. Toss with the dressing just before serving.   Serves 8.

5 tomatoes
2 green peppers
2 Spanish onions
   or 1 Spanish and 1 purple onion
1 large English cucumber
½ cup feta cheese (125 mL)
½ cup Calamata olives (125 mL)
salt and pepper

Seed tomatoes and cut into large cubes. Cut pepper into slices or 1-inch (2.5 cm) cubes and onions in quarters, then paper-thin slices. Chop English cucumber into chunks. (If using regular cucumber, peel and seed before chopping.) Pat vegetables dry and layer in salad bowl. Refrigerate until just before serving. Toss vegetables with enough of the dressing to coat well and stir in feta cheese. Decorate top with olives and additional feta cheese.

Dressing

¼ cup white wine vinegar (50 mL)
1 cup olive oil (250 mL)
juice of ½ small lemon
¼ teaspoon Dijon mustard (1 mL)
pinch salt
¼ teaspoon pepper (1 mL)
½ teaspoon basil (2 mL)
½ teaspoon oregano (2 mL)
1 teaspoon chervil (5 mL)
   or 2 tablespoons chopped parsley (30 mL)
½ teaspoon Italian Seasoning (2 mL)
1 clove garlic, pressed

Mix all together in a sealed top jar and shake well. If you prefer a less sharp taste, add more oil. The dressing can be made days ahead and stored in the refrigerator.

Chef on the Run 99

Carrot Cake from Devine

This is everyone's favourite, the basic, traditional carrot cake. I recommend baking it in a 12 by 9-inch (22 x 33 cm) pan to make the cake thinner, more like a square.   Serves 8

 1 cup brown sugar (250 mL)
 1 cup salad oil (250 mL)
 3 large eggs
 1⅓ cups all-purpose flour (325 mL)
 1⅓ teaspoons baking powder (6 mL)
 1⅓ teaspoons baking soda (6 mL)
 pinch salt
 pinch nutmeg
 ¼ teaspoon cinnamon, optional (1 mL)
 2 cups grated carrots (500 mL)
 ½ cup chopped nuts (optional) (125 mL)

Combine sugar and oil in bowl, add eggs one at a time and beat well. Sift dry ingredients and add to the egg mixture. Beat until well blended. Fold in the grated carrots and nuts, pour into greased pan and bake at 350°F (180°C) for about 35 to 45 minutes or until cake tests done with a straw. Frost with Cream Cheese Frosting.

Cream Cheese Frosting
 4 ounces cream cheese, at room temperature (125 g)
 ¼ cup butter (50 mL)
 2 cups icing sugar (500 mL)
 1 teaspoon vanilla (5 mL)
   or orange liqueur

Cream cheese and butter and blend in icing sugar and vanilla or liqueur.

Diane's Health Cookies

These giant cookies are excellent for picnics, to pack along in your hiking rucksack or for everyday munching. They are very good for you! Makes about 2½ to 3 dozen.

1 cup whole wheat flour (250 mL)
1 teaspoon baking powder (5 mL)
pinch salt
¾ tablespoon cinnamon (10 mL)
⅛ teaspoon powdered ginger (0.5 mL)
1½ cups raisins (375 mL)
1 cup walnuts, chopped (250 mL)
1 cup pecans, chopped (250 mL)
½ cup pine nuts, chopped (optional) (125 mL)
1 cup peanuts (salted or not) (250 mL)
½ cup sunflower seeds (125 mL)
½ cup sesame seeds (125 mL)
½ cup wheat germ (125 mL)
1 cup oatmeal (not instant) (250 mL)
1 cup butter (250 mL)
½ cup creamy peanut butter (125 mL)
1¼ cups brown sugar (300 mL)
2 large eggs
¼ cup milk (50 mL)

Combine flour, baking powder, salt, cinnamon and ginger in a large bowl. Add raisins and toss until coated. Add nuts, seeds, wheat germ and oatmeal and mix together. In a separate bowl, cream butter and peanut butter, add sugar and beat well, then add eggs, one at a time. Add milk. Pour butter mixture over dry ingredients and stir well or mix with your hands until dry ingredients are well moistened. Drop by heaping tablespoons 2½ to 3 inches (6 to 7 cms) apart on foil-lined cookie sheet. Flatten cookies slightly. Bake in pre-heated 350°F (180°C) oven for 15 to 18 minutes on the second rack from the bottom until light brown and semi firm to the touch. Transfer cookies with metal spatula to wire racks to cool. They will keep fresh for several days.

Ambrosia Cake

Pineapple and banana give this cake moistness and flavour. Little chunks of banana speckle the cake throughout.   Serves 8.

2 cups brown sugar (500 mL)
1 cup salad oil (250 mL)
3 large eggs
1 8-ounce can crushed pineapple (250 mL)
1½ teaspoons vanilla (7 mL)
2 cups all-purpose flour (500 mL)
1 cup whole wheat flour (250 mL)
pinch salt
1 teaspoon baking soda (5 mL)
1 teaspoon baking powder (5 mL)
½ teaspoon cinnamon (2 mL)
2 cups finely diced banana (500 mL)

In a large mixing bowl, combine sugar and oil. Add eggs, one at a time, beating well after each addition. Blend in pineapple, undrained, and vanilla. In a separate bowl, combine flours, salt, baking powder, soda and cinnamon. Blend into pineapple mixture and stir in the diced (not mashed) bananas. Turn into a greased 10-inch (25 cm) tube pan and bake in a 350°F (180°C) oven for about 60 to 70 minutes or until it tests done with a straw. Cool in the pan for 10 minutes, then remove to a wire rack to cool. When cool, drizzle with orange glaze.

Orange Glaze
1¾ cups sifted icing sugar (450 mL)
2 to 3 tablespoons orange juice (30 to 45 mL)

Mix together, adding only enough juice to make a pouring consistency.

Viva Italia!

Cinzano or Dubonnet-on-the-Rocks
Antipasto Tray
Fettucine alla Papalina
Veal Mozzarella
Butter-baked Rice (page 74)
Eggplant Parmesan
Biscuit Tortoni
Chocolate Almond Velvet
Cheese and Fruit

Invite your friends over for an informal get-together and serve these hearty Italian dishes. Everything can be prepared in stages and there is almost no work to do when your guests arrive. The antipasto tray, prepared in the morning, serves as both the appetizer and the salad course and I also leave it on the table for nibbling during the veal course. The two kinds of ice cream tarts make a refreshing finale to a robust meal.

For a smaller, simpler dinner, leave out the eggplant and rice or fettucine. The fettucine by itself makes a splendid quick meal. Just add a green salad, or antipasto tray.

Antipasto

The way the Italians make it, antipasto is a delicious and eye-catching arrangement of fresh vegetables, olives, ham, melon and whatever the chef feels like serving. You can prepare the tray early in the day and refrigerate until ready to serve. Supply plenty of Italian bread and breadsticks, provide salad plates, forks and napkins and let your guests help themselves. With the addition of fresh shrimp, tuna and cheese, the antipasto makes a light meal by itself, delicious for lunch or dinner on a hot summer evening. These are a few of my antipasto specialties. Use all or a few and vary the quantities to suit the number of guests.

Fresh Relish Italiano
Thinly slice tomatoes, cucumber and onions, separating onions into rings. Put each into separate bowls and marinate in Italian dressing for

30 minutes, then drain. Arrange in a row on serving platter, alternating tomato, onion and cucumber slices and sprinkling with salt, pepper and chopped parsley. Make several rows on platter, alternating them with other items.

Italian Dressing

Combine 4 parts of olive oil with 1 part red or white wine vinegar, 1 clove garlic, crushed; pinches of basil, chervil and oregano; ¼ teaspoon (2 mL) Dijon mustard; juice of ¼ lemon. Shake well.

Avocado Slices with Salami

Dip slices of ripe avocado in bottled tomato French dressing and alternate on tray with thin slices of salami or other sausage such as genoa, mortadella, sopressa, summer or beer.

Olive-stuffed Eggs

Peel 5 hard-cooked eggs and halve them lengthwise. Remove yolks, mash and combine with 2 tablespoons (30 mL) each of mayonnaise and chopped ripe olives, ½ teaspoon (2 mL) wine vinegar, dash of Dijon mustard, salt, pepper and 1 tablespoon (15 mL) chopped parsley. Mound this filling onto the eggs and trim with ripe olive rings and pimento strips.

Melon with Prosciutto

Wrap peeled honeydew melon or cantaloupe wedges with slices of prosciutto ham and secure with toothpicks.

Marinated Artichoke Hearts

Drain 1 or 2 cans of artichoke hearts and cut each heart in half. Place in a bowl. Combine 6 tablespoons (90 mL) each of lemon juice and olive oil, add 1 clove of garlic, crushed, and salt and pepper. Pour over the artichokes and chill for 30 minutes. Arrange on platter, tucking thin slices of lemon in between and sprinkle with paprika.

Add plenty of carrot and celery sticks, radish roses, green onions and lots of large ripe and green spiced olives, plus bread and breadsticks. Italian cheese, such as Paron, Tynbo or Montasio make interesting additions.

Fettucine alla Papalina

All you need to make this outstanding Italian specialty are noodles (fresh if possible), ham, mushrooms and cheese. It takes only about 20 minutes to prepare from scratch. Add a mixed green salad, hot Italian bread and a bottle of Chianti and you have a great meal.   Serves 4 to 6 as entree.

4 tablespoons butter (60 mL)
2 cups fresh mushrooms, sliced (500 mL)
2 cups cooked ham in julienne strips (500 mL)
½ cup finely chopped onion (125 mL)
1 pound fettucine, green or white (500 g)
8 egg yolks
½ cup grated fresh Parmesan cheese (125 mL)
12 tablespoons butter (180 mL)
4 tablespoons Parmesan cheese (60 mL)
4 tablespoons chopped parsley (60 mL)

Melt butter in large skillet and saute mushrooms, ham and onions for 5 minutes until slightly tender and ham is brown. Set aside and keep warm. Cook noodles until *al dente* (soft but still chewy). Beat egg yolks in top of double boiler, add Parmesan cheese, then butter, about 1 table-spoon (15 mL) at a time, blending well. Place egg mixture over hot, not boiling, water and stir constantly over low heat just until butter starts to melt. Do not overcook or mixture will curdle. Take pan off heat and beat mixture with wire whisk until sauce is slightly thick. Drain noodles and place in serving bowl, pour egg mixture over and toss well. Spoon ham mixture over top, sprinkle with 4 tablespoons (60 mL) Parmesan cheese and parsley, toss and serve. Pass additional cheese. This dish also goes well with sauteed zucchini slices.

Veal Mozzarella

This dish is fairly rich so only small portions are needed. For a simpler supper, serve it alone with rice or noodles, salad and Italian bread. It freezes well.

Serves 8.

> 1 cup milk (250 mL)
> 2 large eggs, slightly beaten
> salt and pepper
> 2 pounds veal cutlets (1 kg), sliced ¼-inch (6 mm) thick
> fine dry breadcrumbs
> ½ pound Mozzarella or Monterey Jack cheese, grated (250 g)
> tomato sauce (see below)

Combine milk, eggs, salt and pepper. Dip veal pieces into egg mixture, then into a bowl with bread crumbs, coating them well. Brown veal in about ¼ inch (6 mm) of olive oil in a hot frying pan until golden on both sides and place in a single layer in a shallow baking dish. Pour tomato sauce evenly over the top. At this stage the dish can be frozen for future use; otherwise cover and refrigerate until ready to bake and serve. Bake uncovered at 350°F (180°C) for about 35 minutes until hot and bubbly. Sprinkle cheese on top and bake for an additional 5 minutes or until cheese melts.

Tomato Sauce

> 1 large onion, chopped
> 3 tablespoons finely chopped green pepper (45 mL)
> 1 clove garlic, crushed
> 1 cup freshly sliced mushrooms (250 mL)
> 2 tablespoons olive oil (30 mL)
> 1 5½-ounce can tomato paste (156 mL)
> 1 14-ounce can tomato sauce (398 mL)
> ¼ teaspoon oregano (1 mL)
> ½ teaspoon basil (2 mL)
> 1 teaspoon sugar (5 mL)
> salt and pepper

In a 3-quart (3 L) saucepan saute onion, green pepper, garlic and mushrooms in olive oil until slightly tender. Stir in tomato paste and tomato sauce and add basil, oregano, sugar, salt and pepper. Simmer for about 50 minutes until thick.

Eggplant Parmesan

This eggplant dish is tasty, an excellent complement for roast lamb as well as veal.   Serves 8.

2 medium eggplants
3 large eggs, beaten
2 cups dry breadcrumbs (500 mL)
3 large tomatoes, peeled and cut into small pieces
2 cups fresh bread cubes (500 mL)
1 clove of garlic, crushed
3 tablespoons chopped parsley (45 mL)
pepper and salt
2 tablespoons salad oil (30 mL)
¼ cup grated fresh Parmesan cheese (50 mL)

Peel eggplant, cut into ¼-inch (6 mm) slices then into ¼-inch (6 mm) strips. Place on paper towels, sprinkle with salt and let stand for about 30 minutes. Pat dry. Dip eggplant strips into beaten eggs, then into dry breadcrumbs and saute in about ¼ cup (50 mL) salad oil until golden, adding more oil as needed. Drain well, then arrange in two layers with the tomatoes in shallow baking dish. Combine bread cubes with garlic, parsley, 2 tablespoons (30 mL) salad oil and cheese. Toss well and sprinkle mixture over eggplant. Cover and refrigerate overnight. Next day, heat oven to 350°F (180°C) and bake uncovered for about 25 to 30 minutes until hot and bread cubes are golden.

Biscuit Tortoni

A delightful Italian ice cream dessert, these tarts may be frozen weeks ahead. They are great with fresh strawberries. Almond macaroons should be available in most bakeries.   Makes 12 tarts.

   2 large eggs, separated
   ½ cup icing sugar (125 mL)
   4 tablespoons light rum or medium dry sherry (60 mL)
   ½ teaspoon vanilla (2 mL)
   ½ pint whipping cream, whipped (250 mL)
   ½ cup plus 3 tablespoons crushed almond macaroons (125 plus 45 mL)
   ¼ cup maraschino cherries, drained and chopped (50 mL)

Beat egg yolks with sugar until fluffy. Stir in rum or sherry and vanilla. Beat egg whites until stiff and fold into yolks, then fold in the whipped cream, ½ cup (125 mL) macaroons and cherries. Put medium-size paper cups into muffin tin and fill each ¾ full with the mixture. Sprinkle with remaining macaroons and freeze, uncovered, until solid. Place in tightly-lidded freezer tin and seal well. Serve frozen.

Chocolate Almond Velvet

This ice cream dessert is really easy to make and so popular. I always keep some on hand for Christmas entertaining as the frozen tarts are a welcome change from rich fruitcakes and mincemeat pies. They are also a real hit at children's parties.   Makes 24.

1 10-ounce can chocolate syrup (284 mL)
1 pint whipping cream (500 mL)
1 can sweetened condensed milk
½ teaspoon vanilla (2 mL)
½ cup toasted slivered almonds (125 mL)
½ cup toasted almonds, crushed (125 mL)

Combine chocolate syrup, cream, condensed milk and vanilla and chill in refrigerator for about 1 hour. Whip until fluffy and mixture forms soft peaks. Fold in the slivered nuts. Put paper cups in muffin tins and fill each ¾ full with the mixture. Top each with crushed nuts and freeze, uncovered until firm. Store in airtight freezer container until needed. Decorate each with a stemmed cherry to serve and do not bring out from the freezer too soon before serving for they melt quickly.

Canadiana Favourites

Alaska King Crab Legs
and
B.C. Prawns
with
Hot Devilled Butter
and Piquant Dip
French Canadian Tourtière
Sour Cream Sauce
Maritime Baked Beans
Fiddleheads and Smoked Salmon Salad
Maple Oatmeal Bread
Canadian Cheese Plate
Chocolate Pound Cake with
Raspberry sherbert or Fresh Raspberries
Blanc de Blanc white wine

This cross-Canada menu would be great to serve on Boxing Day or New Year's Eve when everyone is tired of turkey. The tourtière by itself would also make a nice light meal along with a tossed salad, French bread and assorted cheeses. Crab legs and prawns are served with two dips, one hot, one cold. (These are optional extras and may be deleted.) The tourtière is accompanied by home-baked beans and a salad of marinated fiddleheads and smoked salmon. For dessert, there's a chocolate pound cake, to be served alone or with raspberry sherbert or fresh raspberries.

Crab Legs and Prawns

Allow one large crab leg per person, and three or four prawns. Thaw crab legs about two to three hours before serving, then heat on rack for 8 minutes per side in 350°F (180°C) oven until heated through. If prawns are raw, peel, leaving tails intact, put into saucepan, cover with water and bring to boil. Simmer for 5 minutes until prawns turn pink. Drain, sprinkle with lemon juice and seasoned salt and keep warm. Arrange hot seafood on large platters with sauces for dipping and bread in decorative baskets.

Hot Devilled Butter

½ cup butter (250 mL)
2 teaspoons prepared mustard (10 mL)
1 teaspoon Worcestershire Sauce (5 mL)
2 tablespoons chili sauce (30 mL)
dash tabasco
4 teaspoons lemon or lime juice (20 mL)
1 tablespoon chopped parsley (15 mL)
pinch garlic salt

Melt butter and add rest of ingredients and heat until bubbly. Keep warm in chafing dish.

Piquant Dip

2 cups mayonnaise (500 mL)
¼ cup light cream (50 mL)
2 tablespoons lemon juice (30 mL)
2 teaspoons white wine vinegar (10 mL)
¼ teaspoon dry mustard (1 mL)
½ teaspoon salt (2 mL)
2 tablespoons chopped chives (30 mL)
3 hard-cooked eggs, coarsely chopped
1 dill pickle, chopped

Combine in order given, folding eggs in gently. This dip also makes a good dressing for a chef's salad.

French Canadian Tourtière with Sour Cream Sauce

This delectable adaptation of the classic Quebec Tourtière can be made and frozen baked or unbaked weeks ahead of serving. Thaw overnight and bake as directed. The sour cream pastry is exceptionally good.

Serves 6 to 8.

Pastry

> 2 ½ cups white flour (625 mL)
> ½ teaspoon salt (2 mL)
> 12 tablespoons chilled butter (180 mL)
> 1 large egg
> ½ cup sour cream (125 mL)

Filling

> 3 tablespoons butter (45 mL)
> ½ onion, finely chopped
> 1 cup chopped mushrooms (250 mL)
> 2 pounds ground meat
>   (combination of beef, pork and veal) (1 kg)
> ¼ cup parsley, finely chopped (50 mL)
> ¼ teaspoon salt (1 mL)
> pinch pepper
> ⅛ teaspoon savoury (0.5 mL)
> ⅛ teaspoon ground cloves (0.5 mL)
> ¼ teaspon celery salt (1 mL)
> ½ cup milk (125 mL)
> ½ cup fine dry bread crumbs (125 mL)
> 1 egg, slightly beaten
> 1 cup medium Cheddar cheese, grated (250 mL)

Mix flour and salt in a bowl, add small pieces of butter and blend until it flakes. Mix egg and sour cream and add to flour mixture. Form into a ball, wrap in wax paper and store in refrigerator. This can be made two days ahead of making the pie. Cut the chilled dough in half and roll each section out to form rectangles 6 by 14 inches (15 x 35 cm). (Make one piece slightly larger.) Butter a flat cookie sheet. Place smaller rectangle on top of cookie sheet, place prepared meat mixture in the centre, patting it into a long narrow loaf and leaving a border all around of about ⅓ inch (1 cm). Brush edges with mixture of 2 egg yolks plus 1 tablespoon (15 mL) water, then top with remaining pastry. Press all edges down with the back of a fork to seal well. Prick or slash the top and decorate with a lattice of leftover pastry cut into ¼-inch strips. Brush pie all over with remaining yolk mixture. At this stage the pie may be wrapped, sealed and frozen or refrigerated overnight. Bake in 375°F (190°C) oven for 45 minutes or until golden brown. If pastry becomes too brown, cover with foil. Serve with Sour Cream Sauce.

To make meat filling, melt butter in skillet, saute onions and mushrooms until tender. Set aside. Add meat to skillet and saute until browned. Remove excess fat, leaving only 1 tablespoon (15 mL). Return onions and mushrooms to the pan and add seasoning, milk, breadcrumbs, egg and cheese. Simmer over low heat for about 3 minutes. Refrigerate about 20 minutes or until cold.

Sour Cream Sauce

2 cups sour cream (500 mL)
1 tablespoon Dijon mustard (15 mL)
1 tablespoon chopped parsley (15 mL)

Combine all ingredients. Serve at room temperature. Makes 2 cups.

Maritime Baked Beans

There is nothing tastier than a crock of home-baked beans just out of the oven. This recipe comes from the Maritimes where I grew up and I think it is one of the most flavourful I have ever eaten. Beans go well with barbecued steaks and hamburgers for summer entertaining. They can be made two or three days ahead of serving, and any leftovers freeze well.

Serves 12 to 16

6 cups small white beans (1.5 L)
2 celery stalks, cut in half
½ cup chopped parsley (125 mL)
1 small onion, peeled and studded with 6 cloves
1 clove garlic, crushed
pinches of oregano, thyme, chili powder and salt
water
¾ pound salt pork or side bacon (375 g)

Stock

4 to 5 cups reserved bean stock (1 to 1.25 L)
½ cup chili sauce (125 mL)
½ cup tomato ketchup (125 mL)
5½-ounce can tomato paste (156 mL)
1 cup molasses (not blackstrap)
¾ cup brown sugar (200 mL)
½ teaspoon dry mustard (2 mL)
pepper and salt
dash of Worcestershire Sauce

Put beans in large Dutch oven and cover beans with water to a depth of at least 5 inches (12 cm). Add celery, parsley, onion, and seasonings, bring to boil and simmer for 1½ to 2 hours until beans are tender. Do not overcook. Remove pot from heat, take out beans and place in bowl. Chop up celery and onion and add to bowl. Discard cloves but save all the bean stock. Cut salt pork in small cubes and rinse it in water to remove excess salt. Place beans in bean crock in layers with chunks of pork or bacon and store in refrigerator.

Combine 4 to 5 cups (1 to 1.25 L) of reserved stock with rest of stock ingredients and store in refrigerator. When ready to bake, pour stock over the beans in the crock just to cover. If you need more stock, use more of the reserved stock or use water. Seal lid well with foil, and bake at 250°F (120°C) for about 8 hours until thick but still moist. About half an hour before it is ready, remove cover and stir in ½ cup (125 mL) of medium dry sherry and sprinkle top with a layer of brown sugar.

Fiddleheads and Smoked Salmon Salad

This is an unusual salad, a combination of Maritime fiddlehead ferns and B.C. smoked salmon. If frozen fiddleheads are not available, you can substitute asparagus spears, preferably fresh.   Serves 6 to 8.

1 cup olive or salad oil (250 mL)
¼ cup red wine vinegar (50 mL)
¼ cup lemon juice (50 mL)
1 small garlic clove, crushed
dash of Worcestershire Sauce
pinches of basil, tarragon and dry mustard
1 teaspoon salt (5 mL)
pepper to taste
2 packets frozen fiddleheads, cooked
5 tomatoes, sliced
2 onions, cut into rings
smoked salmon or lox, sliced paper thin

Make marinade from first eight ingredients. Pour half over the fiddle-heads and half over a mixture of the tomato and onion slices. Leave to marinate for about an hour. Before serving, line a platter with lettuce, arrange drained fiddleheads in centre and tomatoes and onions on either side. Garnish with rolled slices of smoked salmon.

Maple Oatmeal Bread

This is an easy one to make. You don't have to knead it at all — it's all done in the electric mixer.

Makes one round loaf

1¼ cups milk (300 mL)
4 tablespoons butter (60 mL)
1 cup oat flakes (250 mL)
1 envelope dry yeast
¼ cup very warm water (50 mL)
⅓ cup maple syrup (75 mL)
1 egg
1½ teaspoons salt (7 mL)
¾ cup whole wheat flour (200 mL)
2 cups white flour (500 mL)
additional oat flakes

Combine milk and butter in saucepan and heat to boiling. Pour over the oat flakes in a large bowl and cool to lukewarm. Sprinkle yeast into warm water, add 1 teaspoon syrup (5 mL) and leave until bubbly and almost double in volume (about 10 minutes). Add rest of ingredients except for additional oat flakes and 1 cup (250 mL) of the white flour to oatmeal milk mixture, along with risen yeast. Beat with electric mixer at medium speed for 3 minutes to make a soft dough. Add additional cup (250 mL) of white flour and beat well with wooden spoon. Turn into buttered 6-cup (1.5 L) casserole dish, sprinkle with extra oat flakes, and let rise in warm place until double in volume — about 45 minutes. Dough should come an inch (2.5 cm) above the top of the dish. Bake at 350°F (180°C) for about 50 minutes or until loaf sounds hollow when tapped. If loaf browns too quickly, cover with foil. Cool in casserole for 10 minutes, then remove to wire rack. Serve warm. This bread freezes well.

Jack's Chocolate Pound Cake

This moist cake is one of my most requested recipes and our friend Jack Taunton's favourite. It always brings rave comments, from men in particular. It takes minutes to make — but it will disappear in seconds! It freezes well.   Serves 10 to 12.

4 ounces sweet chocolate (125 g)
2¾ cups cake flour (700 mL)
1¾ cups white sugar (450 mL)
1 teaspoon salt (5 mL)
¾ teaspoon cream of tartar (4 mL)
½ teaspoon baking soda (2 mL)
¼ teaspoon cinnamon (1 mL)
1 cup butter, softened (250 mL)
¾ cup milk (200 mL)
1 teaspoon vanilla (5 mL)
3 eggs
1 egg yolk

Melt chocolate and cool. Sift dry ingredients and add to softened butter along with milk and vanilla. Mix well to dampen flour, then beat for 2 minutes in electric mixer. Add eggs, yolk and melted chocolate and beat for another minute. Grease a 10-inch (25 cm) tube or bundt pan, pour in batter and bake at 350°F (180°C) for 50 minutes or until done. Cool 15 minutes in pan, remove, then glaze top and sides with 4 ounces (125 g) of sweet chocolate melted with 1 tablespoon (15 mL) butter, ¼ cup (50 mL) water and blend well with 1 cup (250 mL) icing sugar.

   Serve cake with raspberry sherbert and fresh raspberries or any other ice cream and fresh fruit.

Romantically French

Kir or Champagne
Flaming Spinach Salad
Caviar Pie
Salmon in Brioche Dough
Beurre Blanc Sauce
Zucchini au Gratin
Carrots in Vermouth
Wild Rice with Pine Nuts
La Bouchee Douce
Kahlua Mousse in Chocolate Cups (page 36)
White Chablis, Chardonnay or Riesling
Red Bordeaux or Cabernet Sauvignon

One year 36 students from my cooking school virtually took over La Varenne, the prestigious French cooking school in Paris. For a week we studied at practical kitchen sessions and enjoyed demonstrations in the art of cooking with master chefs showing us their secrets as well as the newest trends in European cuisine. The highlight of the session was when we presented our culinary creations for the chef's approval. We worked in teams of eight, with one chef, four assistants and two apprentices to help. Even so, we were glad the chef was never too critical of our efforts and put us right at ease.

Back in Canada, without an experienced staff to help, putting on a French dinner comparable to those we enjoyed at La Varenne became a challenge. But I finally put together this menu, as elegant as one could wish, very tasty and easy for one person to do alone. All preparation procedures have been simplified and most can be done days — even weeks — ahead. The brioche dough can be stashed in the freezer; the salad, vegetables and desserts get a head start the day before; the salmon is finalized in the morning, leaving only the flaming of the salad and the butter sauce for the last minute. Rice is not really necessary with this dinner but if you do serve it, small portions will suffice.

Flaming Spinach Salad

Spectacular! A flambéed salad is a delight for the eyes and this one also has a unique sweet and sour taste. Men love it!   Serves 6 to 8.

3 10-ounce (300 g) bags of fresh spinach
1 pound bacon (500 g)
¾ cup reserved bacon drippings (200 mL)
⅓ cup red wine vinegar (75 mL)
juice of 1 lemon
4 tablespoons white sugar (60 mL)
½ teaspoon Worcestershire Sauce (2 mL)
¼ to ½ teaspoon Dijon mustard (1 to 2 mL)
2 ounces brandy (60 mL)
3 hard-cooked eggs
toasted sunflower seeds

Remove stems from spinach, wash and dry well and store in sealed plastic bags in refrigerator. (It will keep fresh for two or three days.) Make dressing as follows: Fry bacon until crisp, drain off fat, chop into small squares and refrigerate. Combine ¾ cup (200 mL) of the bacon fat with all the rest of the ingredients (except brandy and eggs) and store in container in refrigerator.

On the day of serving, at the very last minute, break spinach leaves into bite-sized pieces and divide among 6 to 8 salad bowls. In the kitchen, mix the dressing in a skillet with the chopped bacon and heat until very hot. Pour into a chafing dish to bring to the table and keep hot over a candle. Heat brandy in a small saucepan until it begins to vaporize then take it into the dining room, pour it very slowly over the hot dressing and set it alight. Pour about 3 tablespoons (45 mL) of the flaming dressing over each salad and decorate with slices of egg and toasted sunflower seeds.

Caviar Pie

This is an unusual and flamboyant way to serve the most elegant of appetizer foods. Lumpfish caviar is the poorman's version, priced under $5 a tin, but the effect is just as stunning as the more expensive variety.   Serves 12 to 16.

2 to 3 ripe avocados, peeled and thinly sliced
6 hard-cooked eggs
4 tablespoons green onion, finely chopped (60 mL)
5 to 6 tablespoons mayonnaise (75 to 90 mL)
¼ teaspoon Dijon mustard (1 mL)
2 tablespoons chopped parsley (30 mL)
   or 1 teaspoon chervil (5 mL)
half a lemon
salt and pepper
1½ cups sour cream (approx.) (375 mL)
1 3½ ounce tin lumpfish caviar, drained well (99 g)

Dip the sliced avocado in lemon juice and arrange on the bottom of a quiche or pie plate. Mash the cooked eggs and combine with the green onion, mayonnaise, mustard, parsley and salt and pepper to taste. Spoon an even layer over the avocados, then blend sour cream with additional ⅓ teaspoon (1 mL) Dijon mustard and spread this over the top. There should be about ¼-inch (6 mm) layer of sour cream. Sprinkle top with caviar, cover and chill for several hours. Serve with crackers. Guests spoon the creamy pie onto the crackers for nibbling.

Salmon in Brioche Dough

This French entrée is a sensational way to serve salmon. The rich, buttery yet light dough keeps the salmon moist and retains the delicate flavour of the fish and its mushroom stuffing. The tart butter sauce is a perfect accompaniment. Although the recipe sounds long and involved it is really uncomplicated to prepare. The brioche dough is foolproof and easy to handle. This presentation was always a success with my cooking school students.   Serves 12.

Brioche Dough

  2 packages (2 tablespoons) dry yeast (30 mL)
  1/2 cup very warm water (125 mL)
  3 beaten eggs at room temperature
  1/3 cup butter, melted (75 mL)
  1/3 cup salad oil (75 mL)
  4 cups all-purpose flour (1 L)
  3 tablespoons sugar (45 mL)
  1/2 teaspoon salt (2 mL)

Dissolve yeast in warm water. In a medium bowl combine eggs, butter and oil, add yeast and mix well. In a large bowl, mix together 2 cups (500 mL) of the flour with sugar and salt. Add the yeast/egg mixture and beat well with wooden spoon. Stir in 1½ cups (375 mL) more of flour to make a soft dough. Sprinkle the remaining flour onto pastry board, turn out dough and knead the flour in until the dough is smooth and elastic — about 5 minutes. Place in greased bowl, turning once to coat both surfaces, cover with a damp cloth and leave to rise in a warm place for 1½ hours or until doubled. Punch down, wrap well and freeze. (It will keep well for several weeks.) The night before serving, place frozen dough, still wrapped, in refrigerator to thaw. If not freezing dough, make it the day ahead and refrigerate, well wrapped, overnight.

Salmon Filling

> 2 boned salmon fillets, tail ends (each 1½ pounds) (750 g)
> 12 ounces fresh mushrooms, finely chopped (375 g)
> 2 shallots or green onions, chopped
> 3 tablespoons butter (45 mL)
> 1 teaspoon lemon juice (5 mL)
> ¾ cup dry bread crumbs (200 mL)
> 2 tablespoons chicken broth (30 mL)
> 1 egg yolk, beaten
> ½ teaspoon chervil (2 mL)
>   or 2 tablespoons chopped parsley (30 mL)
> salt and pepper
> 2 hard-cooked eggs, shells on
> 1 egg beaten with 1 tablespoon water

Trim salmon fillets to equal sizes. (If you order the fish from a fish market, this will be done for you.) Refrigerate. On the day before serving, saute the mushrooms and shallots in butter, stirring constantly for about 3 minutes. Sprinkle with lemon juice and drain off any excess juice. Add bread crumbs, chicken broth, beaten egg yolk, chervil or parsley, salt and pepper. Cook, stirring, until thickened, then remove from heat, cover and refrigerate overnight.

Cover a large baking sheet without sides with buttered tin foil. Remove brioche dough from refrigerator and punch down. Reserve a small piece for top and bottom fins and roll out half the rest on a floured surface to a rectangle 2 inches (5 cm) longer and 1½ inches (3 cm) wider than the fish fillets. Transfer dough to baking sheet. Place one fillet, smooth side down, in the centre of the dough and place the two eggs in front of the wide end to make a head. Spread mushroom filling evenly over the fillet and top with the second fillet. Brush edges of dough with egg/water mixture and bring the bottom edges up around the sides of the fish and the eggs, pressing down well. Roll out the rest of the dough to a rectangle 3 inches longer and wider than the fish and place on top. Tuck the edges under the bottom dough, and seal well. Round the head end over the hard-cooked eggs. At the opposite end, form a tail by shaping the dough into a triangle and propping it up with a piece of buttered foil. Roll out reserved dough, cut it into 2 triangular fin shapes and press to sides of fish, sealing in place with egg mixture. Pattern the dough surface with a small round cutter to make scales and mark fins and

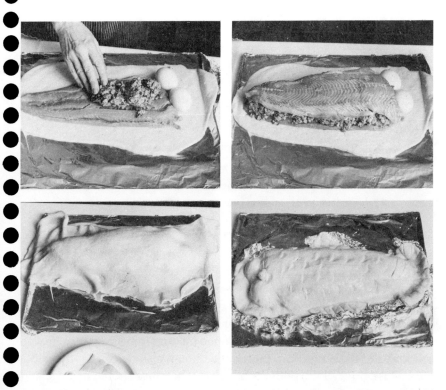

Salmon fillets are placed on brioche dough, sandwiched with a mushroom stuffing, covered with more dough and shaped into a fish form. Fins, tails and scales add surface decoration. Hard-boiled eggs (use two or three) provide shape for the head.

tail with knife, being careful not to cut through the dough. Glaze the entire fish with egg/water mixture and refrigerate. Bake at 350°F (180°C) for about 50 to 60 minutes until golden. If it browns too quickly, cover it with tin foil. Garnish with watercress and lemon wedges. Cut into slices and serve with Beurre Blanc Sauce.

Beurre Blanc Sauce

One of the most outstanding of all French sauces, this one is well worth the extra effort. It is important that the sauce be made at the very last minute, but it takes only about four minutes so it can be done in the kitchen while the guests are relaxing between courses.   Makes 2 cups.

⅔ cup dry white wine (150 mL)
⅔ cup white wine vinegar (150 mL)
4 tablespoons shallots, finely chopped (60 mL)
*   or 4 tablespoons white ends of green onions (60 mL)*
salt and pepper
2 cups butter, cut into 24 pieces (500 mL)

Start the sauce the morning of serving by cooking the wine, vinegar, shallots and salt and pepper in a small heavy saucepan for about 15 minutes or until reduced to about 12 tablespoons (200 mL). Watch closely because the liquid will evaporate quickly. Set aside.

Just before serving, heat reduced wine mixture to boiling, turn heat to low and add the butter, two pieces at a time, whisking constantly with a wire whisk until all the butter is blended. The sauce should be thick and yellow, the consistency of hollandaise sauce. As soon as all the butter is blended, remove from the heat and serve immediately. Don't worry if the sauce cools for the hot salmon will warm it. Do not attempt to reheat it or the whole thing will turn to melted butter.

Zucchini Au Gratin Gourmet 8

This vegetable dish with its delicious crunchy topping is also excellent with lamb and chicken. Prepare it the day ahead and reheat just before serving.   Serves 10 to 12.

4 to 5 zucchini in ¼-inch slices (6 mm)
butter
½ pint sour cream (250 mL)
4 tablespoons butter (60 mL)
2 tablespoons grated Parmesan cheese (30 mL)
salt and pepper
2 egg yolks, well beaten
2 tablespoons green onion (30 mL)
½ cup dry bread crumbs (125 mL)
2 tablespoons melted butter (30 mL)
⅓ cup grated Parmesan cheese (75 mL)

Saute zucchini in butter until barely tender, adding more butter as needed. Do not overcook. Place in shallow 2-quart (2 L) casserole. Blend sour cream, butter, 2 tablespoons (30 mL) cheese, salt and pepper in saucepan and cook gently over low heat until cheese is melted. Remove from heat and add egg yolks and green onions. Pour this mixture over the zucchini. Blend bread crumbs and melted butter and sprinkle over, along with the rest of cheese. Refrigerate overnight. Bake at 350°F (180°C) for about 30 minutes.

Carrots in Vermouth

The vermouth, sugar and butter give the carrots a lift.   Serves 8 to 10.

2 pounds carrots in julienne strips (1 kg)
4 stalks celery, finely sliced on diagonal
1 small red or white onion, finely chopped
⅓ cup sugar (75 mL)
2 tablespoons butter (30 mL)
¾ to 1 cup dry vermouth (200 to 250 mL)

Place vegetables with sugar, butter and vermouth in saucepan and cook over low heat for about 25 minutes until vegetables are slightly tender.

Wild Rice with Pine Nuts

This rice dish can be prepared the day ahead as it reheats beautifully. It is excellent with any roast and as a stuffing for game birds.   Serves 6 to 8.

½ cup pine nuts or filberts (125 mL)
1 cup wild rice, uncooked (250 mL)
2 cups chicken stock (500 mL)
3 tablespoons parsley, chopped (45 mL)
2 tablespoons grated Parmesan cheese (30 mL)
pinch rosemary
salt and pepper

Toast nuts in a 350°F (180°C) oven for about 8 minutes or until golden. Cool, cover and refrigerate. Cook the wild rice in a covered pot in boiling salted water to cover for 5 minutes. Remove from heat and let stand for about an hour. Drain and place in casserole dish. Heat chicken stock until boiling and pour over the rice. Mix in toasted nuts, parsley, cheese, rosemary, salt and pepper and bake in 350°F (180°C) oven for about 45 to 50 minutes or until all the liquid is absorbed. If cooking the day ahead, cool and refrigerate overnight. Reheat at 350°F (180°C) for about 35 minutes or until hot. Any leftovers can be frozen for future use.

Romantically French, page 118, photographed at the home of Peter and Joan Cundill.
Overleaf: Viva Italia, page 103, left. Right, Canadiana Favourites, page 110.

La Bouchee Douce

This "sweet mouthful" is one of my star performers, an instant success each time it is served. It literally melts in the mouth. Leave the assembly until a few hours before serving so the meringue stays crisp, and serve it in your prettiest glass bowl.   Serves 8 to 10.

12 small meringues, about 2 inches in diameter
1 6-ounce package semi-sweet chocolate chips (170 g)
3 tablespoons water (45 mL)
2 pints whipping cream (1 L)
⅔ cup icing sugar (150 mL)
3 tablespoons Cointreau or other orange-flavoured liqueur (45 mL)
2 or 3 cups fresh strawberries, sliced
3 kiwi fruit, peeled and sliced, optional
a few whole strawberries for garnish

Break the meringue into large chunks. Add water to chocolate chips and melt over hot water, stirring until smooth. Whip cream with icing sugar and liqueur until stiff. Spoon a thin (¾ inch) (2 cm) layer of cream in bottom of serving bowl. Cover with a layer of meringue pieces and drizzle meringue with a thin coating of melted chocolate. Put a layer of sliced strawberries and kiwi fruit on top and spread with another layer of whipped cream. Repeat layers, ending with a topping of whipped cream. Decorate with whole strawberries.

Emergency Shelf to the Rescue

Dubonnet on the rocks
Smoked Salmon Mousse with Crackers
Shrimp-stuffed Avocado
Rock Cornish Game Hens
with Wild Rice Stuffing
and Amaretto-Apricot Sauce
Pea Pods Chinese Style
Bananas Flambe
White Burgundy or Chablis wine

"Come for dinner tomorrow". How easy the invitation is given. It is only when you put down the phone that you begin to panic: "What shall I serve?" and "I just don't have time for shopping." This last minute dinner party for four is designed for just those impromptu occasions. And all you have to do — besides keeping calm — is to stock an emergency shelf with the necessary ingredients so you're ready to go into action at a moment's notice.

Besides household staples such as coffee, butter, vinegar, etc., here's what you'll need for "emergency" supplies. Everything on the list, except for a few perishables, will keep well, either in the freezer or on the shelf.

Emergency List
  Dubonnet
  2 or 3 bottles dry white wine
  white rum
  Amaretto liqueur
  Kahlua liqueur
  1 pound soft cream cheese
  6 slices (approximately 3 ounces) smoked salmon
  1 small jar lumpfish caviar
  2 rock Cornish game hens

1 14-ounce can "Oh Canada" wild rice (398 mL)
1 14-ounce can apricots (398 mL)
slivered almonds
2 packages Chinese pea pods, frozen
1 small tin water chestnuts
1 8-ounce jar apricot jam (250 mL)
mushrooms, fresh or canned
shallots or green onions
parsley
onions, white and red
firm bananas
lemons
oranges
2 medium avocados
1 lime
baby shrimp, fresh or frozen
ripe olives

Smoked Salmon Mousse

I always keep a supply of smoked salmon in the freezer and cream cheese in the refrigerator for this last minute appetizer. Thaw the salmon in the morning.
Serves 6 to 8.

1 pound soft cream cheese, room temperature (500 g)
6 thin slices smoked salmon
¼ teaspoon lemon juice (1 mL)
⅛ teaspoon Dijon mustard (0.5 mL)
pepper
2 tablespoons chopped green onions, optional (30 mL)
2 tablespoons chopped parsley, optional (30 mL)
1 small tin lumpfish caviar, optional

Blend the cheese, salmon and all other ingredients except for caviar in a food processor, keeping some of the salmon for garnish. Put into an attractive dish or shell and sprinkle with pieces of reserved salmon. Decorate with thin lemon wedges and parsley and serve with crackers. If you prefer a more subtle flavour, reduce the amount of salmon. To be extra fancy, sprinkle a little of the drained lumpfish caviar on top.

Shrimp-Stuffed Avocado

This makes a tasty change from shrimp cocktail. Have everything ready and add the avocado at the very last moment.   Serves 4.

Sauce
>   4 tablespoons olive oil or salad oil (60 mL)
>   ½ teaspoon Dijon mustard (2 mL)
>   2 tablespoons chili sauce (30 mL)
>   1½ tablespoons wine vinegar (25 mL)
>   dash of Worcestershire Sauce
>   salt and pepper to taste

Combine all ingredients well and store in a covered container in the refrigerator. It will keep for several days.

>   2 medium avocados, not overripe
>   1 tablespoon lime or lemon juice (15 mL)
>   ⅓ to ½ pound baby shrimp, cooked (150 to 250 g)
>   pimento strips
>   ripe olives
>   Butter or Romaine lettuce
>   thin lemon wedges

Halve the avocados lengthwise and discard the pits. Scoop out the flesh and leave shells intact. Immediately cube the avocado and dip in the lime or lemon juice to prevent discolouration. Add cubes to the sauce, then add the shrimp and divide evenly among the four half shells. Place stuffed avocados on lettuce leaves, decorate with pimento and ripe olive and serve with a lemon wedge on the side. This will keep, covered well with plastic wrap, for an hour or so but try to serve immediately.

Rock Cornish Game Hens, with Wild Rice Stuffing

2 rock Cornish game hens
1 14-ounce can "Oh Canada" wild rice, drained (398 mL)
  or 1 cup raw wild rice, cooked (250 mL)
3 tablespoons butter (45 mL)
¼ cup onion, finely chopped (50 mL)
½ cup sliced mushrooms (125 mL)
1 large stalk celery, chopped
3 tablespoons flour (45 mL)
1 tablespoon chicken stock (15 mL)
salt and pepper to taste
pinch of tarragon
2 tablespoons chopped parsley (30 mL)
twist of lemon
½ cup apricot jam (125 mL)
¼ cup Amaretto (50 mL)
Amaretto-Apricot Sauce (see below)

Clean the hens and pat dry. Rub insides with salt if desired. Rinse the wild rice. In a skillet, melt the butter and lightly saute the onions, mushrooms and celery. Blend in flour and cook for one minute. Add the rest of ingredients, except for the jam and Amaretto. Spoon this stuffing into the hens, skewer closed and tie the legs. Baste with a little melted butter and refrigerate for up to 24 hours.

About 70 minutes before serving, place birds on a rack in a roasting pan big enough so the birds do not touch each other. Bake at 425°F (220°C) for 30 minutes. Melt apricot jam, blend with Amaretto and baste the birds with the sauce. Continue to roast and baste for about another 35 to 40 minutes or until legs are tender. Do not overbake.

Cut each bird in half and arrange on a platter with parsley or watercress and slices of orange. Pour a little of the Amaretto-Apricot sauce over each to glaze. Pass the remaining sauce.

Amaretto-Apricot Sauce

¼ cup butter (50 mL)
⅓ cup finely chopped shallots (75 mL)
  or white of green onion
¾ cup fresh or frozen orange juice (200 mL)
juice of 1 lemon (or to taste)
3 tablespoons brown sugar (45 mL)
½ teaspoon Dijon mustard (2 mL)
1 cup Amaretto (250 mL)
2 tablespoons cornstarch (30 mL)
1½ cups quartered canned apricots, drained and stoned (375 mL)
½ cup slivered almonds (125 mL)

Melt the butter in a saucepan, add shallots and simmer for a few minutes. Add orange juice, lemon juice, brown sugar and mustard, then blend Amaretto and cornstarch and add to sauce. Simmer for about 15 minutes until sauce thickens slightly and becomes clear. Add apricots. At this stage, sauce may be refrigerated for up to 24 hours. Reheat and add slivered almonds just before serving.

Pea Pods, Chinese Style

2 packages frozen pods
  or 2 cups fresh (500 mL)
1 cup celery, cut on the diagonal (250 mL)
½ cup coarsely chopped red onion (125 mL)
1 small can water chestnuts, thinly sliced
pinch garlic salt and pepper
1 teaspoon sugar (5 mL)
1 tablespoon soya sauce (15 mL)

If pea pods are frozen, rinse in cold water to thaw and pat dry. Saute pods with celery, onion and water chestnuts until just tender.

It saves time to assemble all the vegetables and ingredients first and saute at the last minute. If you do not have water chestnuts, substitute sliced mushrooms and add ½ cup coarsely-chopped salted cashew nuts.

Bananas Flambe

This dessert is simple to prepare, elegant to serve and simply luscious to taste. When I served it to a group of men students in my cooking class one of them said: "Not for me, please. I hate bananas." But I persuaded him to try a little — and he raved! It is now his favourite dessert. The cold vanilla ice cream provides a good contrast to the warm bananas and the sauce. In my house, Bananas Flambe has become the traditional dessert for New Year's Eve — a grand finale to close the year.

4 to 5 tablespoons butter (60 to 75 mL)
3 tablespoons brown sugar (45 mL)
4 bananas
good pinch of cinnamon
6 tablespoons of Tia Maria or Kahlua (90 mL)
8 tablespoons white rum (125 mL)
vanilla ice cream

In a chafing dish at the table, melt the butter and brown sugar. Peel the bananas and slice them lengthwise, then in half. Add bananas to chafing dish and saute them until just slightly tender, turning them once. Do not overcook or they will become mushy. Sprinkle with cinnamon, add coffee liqueur and blend gently.

Warm rum in a small saucepan until it starts to vaporize, then pour over the bananas and flame. Baste with flaming sauce until the flame dies. Serve immediately with a small scoop of ice cream on top, pouring a little of the sauce over each serving. You can alter the quantities of coffee liqueur and rum to suit.

Family Favourites

We all have treasured recipes that we use time and time again and never tire of. Here are 27 of my family favourites — everything from a paper-bag apple pie to scalloped oysters and sinfully rich Christmas rum balls. Some of the recipes were given to me by friends, some are my own concoctions, perfected over the years, while others go back so far in my files that I can't remember where they came from. They are all excellent.

Appetizers, Salads and Dressings

Liptauer Cheese

There are many versions of the classic Liptauer Cheese mould. I think you will enjoy this one which can be served as an appetizer or as dessert with port. At Christmas I like to fill small pottery crocks with the cheese to give to friends.

Serves 20.

1½ pounds cream cheese (750 g)
1 cup soft butter (250 mL)
1 cup sour cream (250 mL)
2 tablespoons chopped green onion (30 mL)
1 small clove garlic, crushed
2 tablespoons Hungarian sweet paprika (30 mL)
salt and pepper

Blend all ingredients by hand or with an electric mixer. (I found that a food processor makes the mixture a little thinner.) Pack into small serving containers or 1 large one and refrigerate. Serve with assorted fresh fruit and crackers. The cheese can be made two days ahead of serving and it will keep fresh for about four or five days. It also freezes well. Whip it slightly before serving if it has been frozen.

Scalloped Oysters

I always include this dish in my holiday entertaining. It can be prepared the day ahead and reheated just before serving. And it will wait patiently over a warming candle for as long as your guests will let it stand!

Serves 16.

1 quart fresh oysters (1 L)
½ cup butter (125 mL)
½ cup flour (125 mL)
1 teaspoon Hungarian sweet paprika (5 mL)
1 small onion, finely chopped
1 clove garlic, crushed
½ green pepper, finely chopped
1 teaspoon lemon juice (5 mL)
¾ teaspoon Worcestershire Sauce (4 mL)
½ cup cracker crumbs (125 mL)

Cut oysters into small pieces and cook for about 4 minutes in their own juice. In a heavy skillet, melt butter, add flour and cook until well blended and light brown. Add paprika, onion, garlic and green pepper and cook for about 4 minutes. Remove from heat and add lemon juice, sauce and cooked oysters. Mix together gently, pour into a baking/serving dish, sprinkle with crackers crumbs and refrigerate for up to 24 hours. Bake at 375°F (190°C) for about 30 to 40 minutes or until hot and bubbly. Serve with thinly sliced rye bread.

Spinach-Shrimp Salad

A creamy and delicate dressing accents crisp spinach leaves and fresh shrimp. A light supper on its own.   Serves 6 to 8.

 3 10-ounce (300 g) bags fresh spinach, cleaned
 ⅓ cup green onions, chopped (75 mL)
 ½ pound fresh baby shrimp (250 g)
 ¼ pound fresh baby shrimp (125 g)
 4 hard-boiled egg whites
 ½ pound bacon, fried crisp and crumbled (250 g)
 1 tablespoon fresh Parmesan cheese (15 mL)
 1 tablespoon toasted sesame seeds (15 mL)

Dressing
 1 clove garlic
 4 hard-boiled egg yolks
 1 cup olive oil or salad oil (250 mL)
 juice of 1 lemon
 1 tablespoon tarragon vinegar (15 mL)
 ½ teaspoon Dijon mustard (2 mL)
 salt and pepper
 ½ teaspoon tarragon (2 mL)
 ½ teaspoon dill weed (2 mL)

Crush garlic in a salad bowl. Mash cooked egg yolks in the bottom of the bowl and add oil, lemon juice, vinegar, mustard and seasonings. Blend well. Just before serving, add spinach, onions, ½ pound (250 g) shrimp and the egg whites, chopped finely. Toss, then add bacon bits, Parmesan cheese and sesame seeds and toss again. Garnish with the ¼ pound (125 g) shrimp.

Crab-Stuffed Mushrooms

Fresh mushroom caps laden with a cheese fondue - crab filling are a delight to serve with cocktails. Make them the morning of serving.

Serves 8 to 10.

28 medium-sized fresh mushrooms
lemon juice
1 8-ounce package cream cheese (250 g)
2 tablespoons sour cream (30 mL)
1 tablespoon chopped green onion (15 mL)
1 teaspoon lemon juice (5 mL)
¼ teaspoon Dijon mustard (1 mL)
1 clove garlic, crushed
¼ cup Gruyere or Emmenthal cheese, grated (50 mL)
½ cup fresh crab meat (125 mL)
Parmesan cheese

Pull stems from mushrooms and wipe them inside and out with a damp cloth. Dry well and rub with a little lemon juice. Whip cream cheese until fluffy and combine with sour cream, onions, lemon juice, mustard, garlic, cheese and crab. Sprinkle with a little Parmesan cheese and place on a cookie sheet. Refrigerate until ready to serve. Bake in a 375°F (190°C) oven for about 10 to 15 minutes or until hot.

Sharon's Caesar Salad Dressing

This is Sharon Woyat's quick but equally good version of the classic Caesar dressing.

Serves 8.

½ cup oil (125 mL)
2 eggs
6 tablespoons lemon juice (90 mL)
½ teaspoon pepper (2 mL)
1 clove of garlic
½ cup Parmesan cheese (125 mL)
1 can anchovies, including oil

Blend well and refrigerate. Serve with a tossed combination of romaine lettuce, sliced mushrooms, cubed avocado and croutons or toasted sunflower seeds.

Chef on the Run 137

Nancy's Salad Dressing

This recipe hails from Nancy Kennedy of Toronto. Its tart combination of yogurt and seasonings will enhance any salad.

¼ cup salad oil (50 mL)
⅓ cup yogurt (75 mL)
1 teaspoon wine vinegar (5 mL)
1 teaspoon lemon juice (5 mL)
⅛ teaspoon Worcestershire Sauce (0.5 mL)
¼ teaspoon Dijon mustard (1 mL)
1 clove garlic, crushed
½ teaspoon white sugar (2 mL)
toasted sesame seeds

Combine everything except sesame seeds and blend well. Pour over a salad of romaine lettuce, chopped green onions, slightly-cooked broccoli spears or asparagus spears. Sprinkle with sesame seeds. Adjust the lemon juice and vinegar quantities to suit.

Light Dinners and Brunches

Steak Sandwich Superb

This open-faced steak sandwich is ideal for a last minute light dinner, served with a tossed salad and a bottle of your favourite wine. The sauce is irresistible — double the quantity if you like lots!   Serves 4.

butter
4 slices French bread, cut ½-inch (1 cm) thick
1½ pounds (750 g) beef tenderloin, cut into four ¾-inch (1.5 cm) slices
salt and pepper
½ cup tawny port (125 mL)
4 tablespoons whipping cream (60 mL)

Melt enough butter to cover the bottom of a heavy skillet and brown the bread on both sides. Wrap in foil and keep warm in a 350°F (180°C) oven. Clean skillet, add more butter to cover the bottom and brown the steak for about 3 to 4 minutes on each side for rare (longer if desired). Season with salt and pepper and keep warm in oven. Stir port into the same skillet and cook until wine is reduced by half. Add cream and simmer for 2 minutes, stirring constantly. Place slices of hot bread on each plate, serve a steak on top and pour over the sauce.

Fried Oyster and Bacon Sandwich

This is my after-track-practice special, a quick open-faced oyster sandwich. Serve it with a green salad and cold beer.   Serves 4.

> 1 4-ounce package cream cheese, at room temperature (125 g)
> ¼ teaspoon sweet Hungarian paprika (1 mL)
> salt and pepper
> 1 teaspoon chopped green onion (5 mL)
> 4 slices French bread, cut ½ inch (1 cm) thick
> 8 slices of bacon, cut in half
> 1 pint fresh oysters (500 mL)
> 1 cup crackers crumbs (250 mL)
> ¼ teaspoon paprika (1 mL)
> 2 beaten eggs
> 6 tablespoons butter (90 mL)

Blend cream cheese, paprika, salt and pepper and onions. Toast the bread, spread evenly with the cheese mixture and wrap in foil. Fry bacon, wrap in foil and set aside. Trim oysters, removing the tough ends and the muscle. Pat dry. Combine cracker crumbs, paprika, salt and pepper to taste. Dip oysters in beaten eggs, then in the cracker crumb mixture. Heat toast and bacon, covered, in a 325°F (170°C) oven while you saute the oysters. In a skillet, melt butter until frothy and saute oysters until golden and cooked. Arrange on cheese-covered toast and garnish each with 4 pieces of crisp bacon. Decorate plates with lemon wedges and parsley.

Flambe Chicken Dip

The combination of port and cream makes a fine sauce for juicy chicken served between slices of fresh French bread. Warmed peach halves stuffed with port wine or blackcurrant jelly make gourmet accompaniments. Serves 6.

1 4½ pound roasting chicken (2 kg)
1 stalk celery, roughly chopped
1 medium onion, cut in half
¼ cup brandy (50 mL)
1½ cups port wine (375 mL)
¾ cup whipping cream (200 mL)

Heat oven to 425°F (220°C). Rub chicken inside and out with salt and place the celery and onion in the cavity. Place chicken on a rack in a small roasting pan and brown in the oven for about 15 minutes. Remove from oven, pour over the warmed brandy and ignite. Baste chicken well with the flaming sauce. Pour over port and cream, sprinkle with pepper and continue to bake at 350°F (180°C) until chicken is cooked. Baste frequently, adding more port and cream if necessary. Carve and serve thin slices on very warm bread with pan juices as a dip.

Runners' Pizza

When Gavin Smart, one of our club runners stayed with us one summer, he concocted this deep dish pizza with wholewheat crust. A salad and a pizza rolled into one, it is scrumptious! Serve it with plenty of cold beer, cider or wine and you have a winner!

Crust

1 cup warm water (250 mL)
1 package rapid-rising yeast
2 teaspoons honey (10 mL)
1 teaspoon salt (5 mL)

1 tablespoon soft butter (15 mL)
2 cups wholewheat flour (500 mL)
¾ cup wheat germ (200 mL)
salad oil

To make the crust: soften yeast in warm water for 5 minutes. Stir in honey, salt and butter. Combine flour and wheat germ, add one half to the yeast mixture and beat. Add the rest of flour mixture and blend well.

Turn out onto a floured board and knead smooth for a few minutes. Flatten and stretch the dough to fit a well-buttered 9 x 13 x 2½ inch (22 x 33 x 6 cm) pan, pressing dough up the sides about 2 inches (5 cm). Leave to rise in a warm place for about 15 minutes, then brush with salad oil and bake at 425°F (220°C) for about 12 minutes, until golden. Cool, then fill and bake, or refrigerate until ready to fill.

Filling

    1 pound ground beef (500 g)
    3 tablespoons salad oil (45 mL)
    salt and pepper
    1 clove garlic, crushed
    4 tablespoons chopped onion (60 mL)
    1 5½-ounce can tomato paste (156 mL)
    1 7½-ounce can tomato sauce (213 mL)
    2 teaspoons basil (10 mL)
    1 teaspoon oregano (5 mL)
    1 teaspoon Italian seasoning (5 mL)
    1 tablespoon chopped parsley (15 mL)
    ½ teaspoon tarragon (2 mL)
    1 cup Parmesan cheese, freshly grated (250 mL)
    1 medium onion, sliced thinly
    1 cup thinly sliced fresh mushrooms (250 mL)
    1 small green pepper, chopped (optional)
    1 medium zucchini, sliced thinly
    2 medium tomatoes, sliced thinly then cut in half
    2 cups Mozzarella cheese, shredded (500 mL)

To make the filling: In a skillet brown the meat in the salad oil along with garlic and onion. Salt and pepper to taste. Drain any excess fat and set aside. In a bowl, combine tomato paste, tomato sauce and herbs. To assemble: Spread ½ cup (125 mL) of the Parmesan cheese over the dough. Spread tomato sauce mixture evenly on top, then sprinkle on the meat mixture and layer the vegetables. Sprinkle with the remaining ½ cup (125 mL) of Parmesan cheese, then top with the Mozzarella cheese. The dish may then be covered and refrigerated until ready to bake. Bake at 425°F (220°C) for about 30 minutes or until hot and the cheese is melted. Cut into squares to serve.

Spinach and Sausage Frittata

I often whip up this omelette-type dish for a Sunday brunch or a light dinner. It is great for emergencies: simply add a tossed salad, fresh croissants, and fruit and you have a complete meal. Serves 6.

4 small Italian or summer sausages, crumbled
2 tablespoons salad oil (30 mL)
1 10-ounce package frozen spinach, thawed and drained (300 g)
1 cup fresh mushrooms, sliced (250 mL)
½ medium onion, chopped
1 clove garlic, crushed
½ cup chopped zucchini (125 mL)
6 large eggs
¾ cup Parmesan cheese (200 mL)
½ teaspoon basil (2 mL)
1 teaspoon chervil (5 mL)
salt and pepper
1 cup grated Mozzarella or Monterey Jack cheese (250 mL)

In a large skillet, saute the sausage over medium heat until cooked. Remove and chop. Drain skillet, add oil and saute spinach, mushrooms, onions and garlic until onions are soft. Remove vegetables and set aside. Add a little more oil to the pan if needed, then saute the chopped zucchini until slightly soft. In a bowl combine eggs with ½ cup (125 mL) of the Parmesan cheese, basil, chervil, salt and pepper and beat well. Add sausage and the vegetables and turn into a 9-inch (22 cm) quiche pan or pie plate. Sprinkle with the Mozzarella cheese and the remaining Parmesan and bake about 25 minutes in a pre-heated 350°F (180°C) oven or until set. Cut into 3-inch (7.5 cm) squares to serve.

Salmon Quiche

This quick supper recipe comes from Thelma and Lee Wright, two former Olympic competitors. The combination of salmon, cheese and dill blended with the tart sour cream and yogurt makes it unique. Serves 4 as main course; 6 for appetizer.

Crust

1 cup wholewheat flour (250 mL)
⅔ cup grated Cheddar cheese (150 mL)
¼ cup chopped toasted almonds (50 mL)
pinch salt
¼ teaspoon paprika (1 mL)
6 tablespoons salad oil (90 mL)

Filling

1 6½-ounce can salmon (184 mL)
3 eggs, beaten
½ cup sour cream (125 mL)
½ cup yogurt (125 mL)
¼ cup mayonnaise (50 mL)
½ cup Cheddar Cheese, grated (125 mL)
1 tablespoon chopped green onion (15 mL)
¼ teaspoon dill weed (1 mL)
3 drops hot pepper sauce (optional)

For the crust, combine dry ingredients, add oil, stir well and press into a 9-inch (22 cm) pie plate. Bake at 400°F (200°C) for 10 minutes, then cool.

For the filling: drain and flake the salmon, reserving the liquid. Blend eggs, sour cream, yogurt, mayonnaise and salmon liquid then fold in salmon, cheese, onions, dill and hot pepper sauce. Spoon into shell and bake at 325°F (160°C) for about 40 minutes or until firm. The cooked quiche can be refrigerated and reheated at 325°F (160°C) for about 30 minutes, or the crust and filling can be made in the morning and kept separate until ready to bake and serve.

Spaghetti Sauce

This is my son Rand's favourite. It's a thick sauce, not too highly seasoned and all the young people love it. My sister-in-law Ruth Matheson of Halifax passed the recipe on to me and other family members across Canada. We all swear by it. Quick to prepare, it can also be used as a sauce for lasagne and it freezes well.

Serves 8

1 10-ounce can beef bouillon, undiluted (284 mL)
1 10-ounce can tomato soup, undiluted (284 mL)
1 5½-ounce can tomato paste (156 mL)
1 14-ounce can spaghetti sauce (398 mL)
2 14-ounce (398 mL) cans tomato sauce
1½ pounds ground beef (725 g)
2 tablespoons salad oil (30 mL)
1 large onion, chopped
1 clove garlic, crushed
salt and pepper
1 teaspoon oregano (5 mL)
1 teaspoon basil (5 mL)
½ teaspoon Italian seasoning (2 mL)
2 teaspoons chervil or chopped parsley (10 mL)
1 teaspoon sugar (5 mL)
pinch of cinnamon

Open the cans, mix together and set aside. Saute the beef in oil in a large Dutch oven and drain excess fat. Add onion, saute until soft, then add rest of ingredients. Bring to boil, stirring, then simmer uncovered at low heat for about 1½ hours or until thick. If desired, add 1 cup (250 mL) sliced mushrooms.

Super-Quick Eggs Benedict

Brennan's Restaurant in new Orleans is famous for its Eggs Benedict brunches served in an elegant courtyard. This particular version of the dish has lots of sauce and it is our favourite after a Sunday morning run. It takes only a few minutes to make but Doug thinks it equals the ones we had at Brennan's — and that's a real compliment! Serves 4.

1½ cups mayonnaise (375 mL)
½ cup sour cream (125 mL)
2 teaspoons lemon juice (10 mL)
1 teaspoon Dijon mustard (5 mL)
salt and pepper
4 eggs
12 slices back bacon
2 English muffins, split in half
paprika

In a saucepan combine mayonnaise, sour cream, lemon juice, mustard, salt and pepper and keep hot over low heat. Poach eggs. Do not over cook them — they should be medium soft. Saute the bacon and toast the muffins. Top muffin halves with bacon slices and egg and smother with hot sauce. Serve with sauteed or grilled tomato slices sprinkled with chopped parsley and Parmesan cheese.

Sweets

Paper Bag Apple Pie

Try baking an apple pie in a paper bag — a new twist to an old favourite. But be careful not to put the bag too close to the oven burners. Large chunks of apple spiced with cinnamon and nutmeg, and a crunchy golden topping make this one of the greatest apple pies of all time.

1 9-inch pie shell, unbaked (22 cm)
8 to 10 cups tart apples, in chunks (2 to 2.5 L)
½ cup sugar (125 mL)
2 tablespoons flour (30 mL)
½ teaspoon cinnamon (2 mL)
¼ teaspoon nutmeg (1 mL)
juice of ½ lemon
½ cup sugar (125 mL)
½ cup flour (125 mL)
½ cup butter (125 mL)

Pare, core and quarter the apples, then halve each quarter crosswise to make large chunks. Combine ½ cup sugar (125 mL) with 2 table-spoons (30 mL) flour, cinnamon and nutmeg and sprinkle over the apples, tossing well to coat. Place in the unbaked pie shell and sprinkle with lemon juice. Combine sugar, flour and butter and sprinkle over the apples to cover. Take a large brown paper grocery bag and wet it thoroughly with water. Place it on a cookie sheet and put the apple pie inside, leaving lots of room between the top of the pie and the bag for the steam to rise. Fold the end of the bag several times and secure with paper clips. Keep it away from oven elements. Bake at 425°F (220°C) for about 45 to 50 minutes. Serve warm with whipped cream flavoured with a dash of cinnamon and icing sugar, or with vanilla ice cream.

Christmas Rum Balls

Without a doubt, these are the best rum balls you could ever make. I never seem to make enough of them at Christmas. I start with 14 dozen to send to friends and relatives across Canada, then make lots more. I also take them to meetings. They are so popular with B.C. Sports Hall of Fame members that they call them their "Executive Rum Balls." The secret of this recipe is the addition of sour cream and almond paste. They produce a confection that is creamy and yummy! Make them weeks ahead and store them in the refrigerator. They need two weeks to mature — if you can wait that long. This recipe makes a large batch — about 9 to 10 dozen.

12 ounces semi-sweet chocolate chips, melted (340 g)
½ cup almond paste (125 mL)
1 cup sour cream (250 mL)
pinch salt
8 cups vanilla wafers, crushed finely (2 L)
3 cups icing sugar (750 mL)
pinch salt
1½ cups melted butter (375 mL)
⅔ cup cocoa (150 mL)
1½ cups white rum (375 mL)
2 cups pecans, finely chopped (500 mL)
chocolate shot or sprinkles

Combine melted chocolate, sour cream, paste and salt. Cream well and set aside. In a separate bowl, combine wafers and the rest of the ingredients except for chocolate shot. Mix until it holds its shape. Add chocolate-sour cream mixture and knead with your hands until blended and soft. Refrigerate until firm enough to form small balls in the palm of your hand, yet soft enough to pick up the chocolate shot. Take tablespoons of the mixture and form into balls then roll in chocolate shot and put on trays lined with wax paper to harden overnight in the refrigerator. Put them into tins and refrigerate. If keeping them for more than 4 weeks, they should be frozen. Take them out of the refrigerator a few hours before serving to soften slightly and bring out the rum flavour.

Giant Blueberry Muffins

These muffins are full of blueberries and have almost a cake-like texture.
They freeze well.

Makes 1 dozen.

2 large eggs
⅔ cup white sugar (150 mL)
½ cup butter, melted (125 mL)
2 cups buttermilk or skim milk (500 mL)
3 cups all-purpose flour (750 mL)
2 tablespoons baking powder (30 mL)
¼ teaspoon salt (1 mL)
1 teaspoon vanilla (5 mL)
3 cups blueberries, fresh or frozen (750 mL)

Heat oven to 400°F (200°C). In a bowl, beat eggs, add sugar and butter and mix well. Stir in the milk. Combine flour, baking powder and salt and beat gently into egg mixture just enough to form a lumpy batter. Do not overbeat. Fold in vanilla and blueberries and spoon into greased muffin pans, filling them almost to the top. Bake for 20 to 25 minutes or until firm. Serve warm.

Mom's Brownies

I remember as a very little girl rushing home from school to make a pan of Mom's brownies — and waiting for Dad's compliments.

½ cup butter (125 mL)
4 squares unsweetened chocolate
2 cups white sugar (500 mL)
2 large eggs
1 cup flour (250 mL)
1 teaspoon vanilla (5 mL)
½ cup finely chopped walnuts (125 mL)

Melt chocolate and butter over low heat. In a medium-size bowl, combine butter mixture and sugar, beat until creamy, then add eggs, one at a time, beating well. Add flour and vanilla and fold in the nuts. Put in a greased 8-inch square (20 cm²) pan and bake at 350°F (180°C) for about 25 to 30 minutes or until just firm to the touch and crusty on top. Do not overbake them: they should be soft and fudgy in the middle. Icing is not necessary, but a chocolate one is always appreciated.

Toasted Almond Shortbread

These tasty shortbread fingers are always part of my Christmas baking. They make a change from traditional shortbread and are a welcome treat at any time of year. They will keep for three to four weeks and can also be frozen. Makes about 2 dozen.

½ pound butter, softened (250 g)
½ cup fruit sugar (125 mL)
1 teaspoon almond extract (5 mL)
¼ teaspoon cream of tartar (1 mL)
2¾ cups pastry flour (700 mL)
    or 2½ cups all-purpose flour (625 mL)
½ cup toasted almonds, finely chopped (125 mL)
16 ounces semi-sweet chocolate, melted (500 g)

In a bowl, cream butter and blend in the rest of the ingredients except nuts and chocolate. Cream well, using your hands to make a stiff dough and adding more flour if needed. Fold in the nuts. Shape into fingers about ¼ inch (6 mm) thick and 3 inches (7 cm) long and curve some of the fingers to form crescents. Do not make them too big as they swell in the oven. Bake at 325°F (160°C) for about 8 minutes or until just golden. Cool, then dip ends into melted chocolate. Put on wire racks to harden. Store in airtight tins, separating layers with foil.

Mincemeat Tart Pastry

This pastry recipe is my favourite for tiny mincemeat tarts. Buy a good mincemeat from a bakery and add a good shot of rum. Makes 2 to 3 dozen tiny tarts.

> 1½ cups pastry flour (375 mL)
> ½ teaspoon baking soda (2 mL)
> ¼ teaspoon salt (1 mL)
> 1 teaspoon cream of tartar (5 mL)
> 2 teaspoons sugar (10 mL)
> ½ cup shortening (125 mL)
> 3 to 4 tablespoons milk (45 to 60 mL)

In a bowl, mix dry ingredients and rub in the shortening. Blend in milk, using more if needed to form a smooth, soft dough. Refrigerate for 10 minutes to make dough easier to handle. Turn onto floured board and roll out. Cut into rounds to line tiny (1½-inch) (4 cm) tart pans. Moisten edges with milk, then fill three quarters full with mincemeat. Top with rounds of pricked pastry just large enough to cover mincemeat and brush tops with milk. Bake at 450°F (230°C) for about 10 minutes or until golden. Cool, store in airtight tins in the refrigerator, or freeze. Reheat in a 350°F (180°C) oven for about 5 minutes and serve with Rum Hard Sauce.

Rum Hard Sauce

This is great with mincemeat tarts and plum pudding. It can be made weeks ahead and stored in the refrigerator but take it out to soften for an hour or so before serving.

> ½ cup butter, softened (125 mL)
> 2 cups icing sugar (500 mL)
> 1 teaspoon vanilla (5 mL)
> ¼ cup white rum (50 mL)

Cream together and refrigerate in a covered jar. Add more rum if desired.

Tia Maria Angel Delight

This is one of my oldest and most frequently used recipes. I keep it filed under "classics!" It happened almost by accident. With company arriving in a few hours, all I had on hand was an angel food cake in the freezer and a few Almond Roca bars. So I dashed out for some whipping cream and put it all together with some coffee liqueur. It was delectable — a great hit with the men. It was featured in our "Gourmet Eight" cookbook.   Serves 12 to 16.

    1 angel food cake
    ¾ cup Tia Maria or Kahlua (200 mL)
    12 small Almond Roca bars
    2 pints whipping cream (1 L)
    3 tablespoons icing sugar (45 mL)
    3 tablespoons Tia Maria or Kahlua (45 mL)

Cut the cake into three layers and lay them out on the counter. Puncture each layer with a skewer and drizzle about ¼ cup (50 mL) of liqueur evenly over each layer. Combine whipping cream with icing sugar and extra coffee liqueur and whip until fluffy. Assemble cake, spreading cream thickly between the layers, on top and over the sides. Refrigerate overnight to let liqueur soak in. In the morning, sprinkle top and sides with crushed Almond Roca bars and decorate plate with fresh strawberries or clusters of grapes. Serve with ice cream if desired.

Porcupines

Whenever sweets were needed for a school or church tea, I was always asked to bring my mother's porcupines. The recipe originated with my aunt Sadie who was in the catering business in Sydney, Nova Scotia. Her porcupines — date-filled tarts frosted with maple icing — were famous throughout the community. Makes 24.

Shortbread Pastry

½ cup butter (125 mL)
¼ cup icing sugar (50 mL)
1 egg yolk
pinch salt
1¼ cups pastry flour (300 mL)

To make the pastry, cream butter and icing sugar then add the rest of the ingredients to make a pliable dough. Line 24 small tart pans and bake at 300°F (150°C) for 12 to 15 minutes. Cool, then remove carefully.

Filling

1 pound dates, chopped (500 g)
⅔ cup brown sugar (150 mL)
1 cup water (250 mL)
1 teaspoon lemon juice (5 mL)

Maple Icing

2 cups brown sugar (500 mL)
½ cup whipping cream (125 mL)
icing sugar
finely chopped walnuts

Combine dates with brown sugar, water and lemon juice and cook over medium heat until mixture is smooth and dates softened. Stir constantly. Cool, then refrigerate before filling tart shells. To make icing, combine sugar and cream in a saucepan, bring to a boil and boil without stirring for 2 to 3 minutes. Cool. Add enough icing sugar to make a spreading consistency — don't make it too stiff. Cover the date filling completely with the icing and sprinkle top with crushed walnuts.

Lemon Filling

The shortbread tart shells for the porcupines can be filled instead with this lemon filling. It is creamy smooth with a subtle flavour. The recipe is my mother's and it is one of the best. Makes filling for 2 dozen small tarts.

6 eggs
½ pound butter (250 g)
1 cup white sugar (250 mL)
juice and rind of 2 lemons
whipped cream

Beat eggs well. Put into a double boiler, add sugar, butter, lemon juice and rind and cook until mixture thickens. Cool and store in a glass jar in the refrigerator — it will keep for at least a week. Fill tart shells just before serving and decorate each with a dollop of whipped cream.

Strawberries Sabayon

A most elegant dessert — the first of the season's sweet strawberries served in wine goblets and drizzled with a smooth Grand Marnier sauce. Serves 6 to 8.

5 egg yolks
½ cup white sugar (125 mL)
2 tablespoons white sugar (30 mL)
¼ cup Grand Marnier (50 mL)
½ pint whipping cream (250 mL)
2 baskets fresh strawberries

Combine egg yolks and ½ cup (125 mL) sugar in a bowl that will fit inside a slightly larger saucepan. Add 2 inches (5 cm) of water to the saucepan and bring to a boil. Beat yolks vigorously with wire whisk, making sure to scrape bottom and sides of the bowl. Place bowl in the saucepan of boiling water (the bottom of the bowl should not touch the water) and continue beating for about 8 minutes or until yolks are thick and pale yellow. Remove bowl from saucepan and stir in half the Grand Marnier. Cool the sauce and chill in the refrigerator. Whip cream with 2 tablespoons (30 mL) sugar until almost stiff. Fold cream into cooled sauce and add the remaining Grand Marnier. Refrigerate until ready to serve. Pile cleaned strawberries in wine goblets and pour sauce over.

Sour Cream Tea Biscuits

These are flaky and moist to compliment a hearty clam chowder or other earthy dish. Without the cheese, the recipe makes a fine shortcake for strawberries.   Makes about 8 biscuits

> 2 cups all purpose flour (500 mL)
> 1 teaspoon white sugar (5 mL)
> ¼ teaspoon salt (1 mL)
> ½ teaspoon baking soda (2 mL)
> 3 teaspoons baking powder (15 mL)
> ½ cup shortening (125 mL)
> 1 cup sour cream (250 mL)
> ¾ cup medium Cheddar cheese, grated (optional) (200 mL)

Preheat oven to 450°F (230°C). Mix the dry ingredients then cut in the shortening until it resembles small peas. Add sour cream and cheese and mix until just blended. Knead about ten times on a lightly floured surface to form a soft, smooth dough. Gently roll out from the centre to ¾-inch (2 cm) thickness and cut into rounds with floured cookie cutter or small glass. Place on ungreased cookie sheet and bake for 10 to 12 minutes until golden. Serve warm for best flavour.

To use for shortcake, omit cheese, add 1 teaspoon (5 mL) sugar and ½ teaspoon (2 mL) vanilla. Bake as biscuits or as one large round and split while hot. Fill with whipped cream, ice cream and fresh, sliced berries.

Old-Fashioned Chocolate Cake

Wendy Robertson O'Donnell, one of Canada's leading marathon runners, makes this cake for us whenever we visit. It is her grandmother's specialty, one of the best chocolate cakes I have ever eaten. It's so moist.

2/3 cup butter (150 mL)
1²/3 cups white sugar (400 mL)
2 eggs
1/2 teaspoon vanilla (2 mL)
   or 1 tablespoon coffee liqueur (15 mL)
pinch salt
1²/3 cups cold coffee (400 mL)
1²/3 cups flour (400 mL)
1/2 cup cocoa (125 mL)
1 teaspoon baking powder (5 mL)
1 teaspoon baking soda (5 mL)

Cream butter and sugar, add eggs one at a time, beating well. Then add flavouring and salt and beat in the cold coffee. Combine flour, cocoa, baking powder and soda and beat gradually into the coffee batter. Pour into an 8 x 12 inch (20 x 30 cm) greased cake pan and bake at 400°F (200°C) for about 15 minutes, then reduce heat to 375°F (190°C) for about 15 more minutes or until done. Cool, then frost with the following:

Icing

1 cup brown sugar (250 mL)
1 egg white
1/4 cup cold water (50 mL)
pinch of cream of tartar
2 tablespoons coffee liqueur (30 mL)

In a double boiler, combine all the ingredients and beat over hot water for about 7 minutes or until thick. Cool and spread on chocolate cake.

Orange Mandarin Mould

Jellied salads are not my favourite but everyone wants the recipe for this tart and tangy mould. It's great for buffets and a hit with the children.

Serves 6.

2 4-ounce (92g) packages orange Jello powder
1½ cups boiling water (375 mL)
12½-ounce tin Minute Maid orange juice, undiluted
2 10-ounce (284 mL) tin mandarin oranges, drained
⅔ cup mandarin orange juice (150 mL)

Dissolve Jello in water, add orange juice and stir well until blended. Add mandarins and juice. Pour into oiled mould and refrigerate overnight. Unmould and serve on lettuce greens decorated with sliced oranges.

Index

Island Salad Bar	60	Rum Cream Torte	78
Joggers' Special	95	Rumaki	52
Kahlua Mousse	36	Rum Hard Sauce	150
Kippered Salmon	90	Runners' Pizza	140
King Crab Fruit Tray	54	Salad Deluxe	92
Kir	30	Salad Nicoise	34
La Bouchee Douce	127	Sharon's Caesar Salad Dressing	137
Lemon Filling	153	Sangria de Granada	44
Lemon Meringue Torte	79	Salmon in Brioche Dough	121
Liptauer Cheese	134	Salmon Quiche	143
Lomi Lomi Salmon Tomatoes	53	Sauteed Zucchini Strips	90
Macadamia Nut Cheese Biscuits	55	Scalloped Oysters	135
Mai Tai Souffle	61	Seafood or Mushroom Pie	33
Maple Oatmeal Bread	116	Shrimp in Feta Cheese	84
Marinated Zucchini Salad	65	Shrimp Istanbul	72
Maritime Baked Beans	114	Shrimp Mousse	6
Mince Meat Tart Pastry	150	Shrimp Stuffed Avocado	130
Mom's Brownies	148	Shrimp Stuffed Red Snapper	58
Mulled Wine	88	Shrimp Thermidor in Croustade	28
Mushrooms, Crab-stuffed	137	Smoked Salmon Mousse	129
Mushrooms, Baked	11	Soupe au Pistou	40
Mushrooms, Stuffed	8	Sour Cream Tea Biscuits	154
Nancy's Salad Dressing	138	Spaghetti Sauce	144
Old Fashioned Chocolate Cake	155	Spiced Apple Sauce	10
Olive Bread	77	Spinach and Sausage Frittata	142
Olive Cheese Puffs	24	Spinach & Shrimp Salad	136
Olive Martini Loaf	8	Spinach Salad, Flaming	119
Onion Soup	42	Steak Sandwich Superb	138
Orange & Avocado Salad	48	Strawberries & Pineapple Grand	
Orange Mandarin Mould	156	Marnier	37
Oriental Meatballs	53	Strawberries Sabayon	153
Paella	47	Stuffed Cherry Tomatoes	7
Pali Punch	52	Suckling Pig	24
Paper Bag Apple Pie	146	Sweet Sour Sauce	54
Pea Pods Chinese Style	132	Tabbouleh Salad	66
Pecan Orange Sweet Potatoes	26	Tia Maria Angel Delight	151
Pineapple Shrimp Boats	55	Toasted Almond Shortbread	149
Piquant Dip	111	Toasted Oatmeal Chocolate Chip	
Polynesian Rice Mingle	57	Cookies	29
Polynesian Sauce	55	Tomatoes with Feta Cheese	82
Potatoes Romanoff	26	Tourtiere	112
Porcupines	152	Tzatziki Sauce	97
Quiche Lorraine Tartlets	23	Veal Mozzarella	106
Raspberry Sauce	29	Vegetable Melange	75
Red Snapper en Papillote	85	Vinaigrette Dressing	76
Rice & Pork Stuffing	25	Wholewheat Loaf	93
Roast Suckling Pig	24	Wild Rice with Pine Nuts	126
Rock Cornish Game Hens	131	Zucchini au Gratin	125
Rum Balls	147	Zucchini Salad, Marinated	65
Rum Cake de Maison	12	Zucchini Strips, Sauteed	90